Here is contemporary man's guide to sanctity, written in modern terms and with a relevance today's Christian can appreciate. A sensitive and creative theologian, Ladislaus Boros asserts that the real pathway to God is through our fellow man. We can accomplish our movement toward divine perfection, he maintains, "in simple straightforward brotherliness, in the humble everyday service of neighbor." The author's insight that God is the absolute in the midst of every human encounter in love, joy, sorrow and suffering, for example, is beautifully stated over and over again. His reflections on such virtues as truthfulness, respect, love, magnanimity, serenity, and honesty—which he uses to draw out the implications of "meeting God in man"—ring with the sincerity of modern men seeking ultimate meaning.

A perceptive and enlightening book, MEETING GOD IN MAN offers the kind of spiritual reading befitting this day and age.

MEETING GOD IN MAN

LADISLAUS BOROS, S.J.

Translated by William Glen-Doepel

IMAGE BOOKS

A Division of Doubleday & Company, Inc.
Garden City, New York

Image Books edition: 1971
by special arrangement with Herder and Herder
Image Books edition published September 1971

Original edition: *Im Menschen Gott begegnen,*
Mainz, Matthias-Grünewald-Verlag, 1967.

Nihil obstat: Francis J. Bartlett, Censor
Imprimatur: ✠Patrick Casey, Vicar General
Westminster, September 23, 1968

CONTENTS

INTRODUCTION

This book is an attempt to resolve the basic tension of Christian life. This can be expressed in two questions which were formulated centuries ago by men who were honestly trying in their own way to be genuine Christians: "How do I find a merciful God?" and "How do I become a real man?"

Martin Luther wrestled all his life with the first problem. This man, who was shaken by God to the depth of his belief, dynamic and violent both in his love and his anger, possessed by the power of the absolute, wrote to Melanchthon from Wittenberg on 27 October 1527: "I am longing and thirsting for nothing but a merciful God." At the same time a sensitive and highly cultivated man, Erasmus of Rotterdam, was trying to find the answer to another question: "How do I achieve genuine (properly founded) humanity?" These two questions were raised in Europe at a time of the most violent upheaval. It was the beginning of the modern age: that age in which we have to find God today. The historical details of the period are too well known for us to list them here, in a theological study. It was the beginning of a new epoch in all areas of human reality. It was a time of the highest stimulation of passions, feelings, knowledge and hopes.

Today too we are living in a time of radical revolution. The change in the whole world of feeling and experience at the present time is so strongly in the consciousness of men that it has already become a commonplace to speak of the "end of the modern period". But we do not want to evoke historical memories here, nor consider what answer and solution the thinkers and seekers we have mentioned thought they had found. In every age of fundamental revolution men will ask exactly the same questions: "How do I find a merciful God?" and "How do I find my way back to my true humanity?" The Christian answer will always lie in this conjunction "and".

I find a gracious God through becoming a real man. To be a Christian means basically that one believes in Christ, that is, in the incarnation of God. God, infinite and ineffable, has become man. For this reason and since then humanity has itself become grace in this God become man. The source of the eternal flows deep within humanity. In the thornbush of the human endeavour to become a real man, the flame of the absolute burns. Since the incarnation of God the divine is always present wherever human life is. The mystery of humanity is bound up essentially with the incarnation of God.

In his incarnation God permeated the whole of human reality. He really became a man. He took on himself the whole of human nature—except for sin—and hence also the terrifyingly normal, the ordinary, the endlessly repetitive and the insignificant, which was part of this nature.

Let us consider for a moment what it means to say that God has become man. God is the name for what is incomprehensible and unnamable. He is that which is absolutely unreachable. It is a particular grace of our time that we are able to experience the "otherness of God" with every fibre of our life. Perhaps this is the only way it can be. Humanity today must pass through the most terrible of all experiences, the distance of God, so that it can again acquire the sense of how radically "other" God really is. Before him all speech, all thought, and all feeling fall silent, and God is he who is "mortally other".

All this is true and yet it is still not quite right. For it is said that God is in the process of *becoming*. This absolute, quite different being, distant and incomprehensible, has placed himself in the situation of touchability, of proximity, of being "like all of us". He became a child, lived an ordinary life among us, learned the trade of a carpenter, wandered about, became tired and weary, and completed his work of redemption in the bloody sweat of fear and the hoarse cry of abandonment. If human thinking breaks down when it tries to conceive "God", how can man even begin to consider the idea of a God that is coming into being!

And then there is the third part of the statement: God

becomes a *man*. In Christ a man full of understanding and goodness appeared among us; someone who took the sinners and the weak under his protection. In Christ "pure humanity" shone forth, for the first time. At last there was a man among us who did not break the broken reed nor extinguish the smoking candle, who constantly said, "Fear not", who proclaimed "the Lord's year of grace", who said to the thief, "Today you will be with me in paradise". Only God could be so human. After this we cannot conceive anything human that cannot be applied to God himself, apart from sin. In Christ God became softened into human charm and goodness.

A little theological reflection will perhaps open up for us yet more deeply the humanity of God. In order to be able to understand, to some degree, the incarnate God, we should remember that in Christ original humanity was fully restored. Theology says, in its abstract language, that Christ lived without "concupiscence". The positive meaning of this negative statement is that Christ has realized his life in the unity of being that originally existed. He was not split between what he was and what he did. He had the capacity of transforming everything he experienced directly into his life. He was in his actions fully "himself". His human nature was totally integrated into his existence (inseparably, but not in a way that the two could be confused). He was wholly man because he was wholly God.

After this there is no other way to God for us men: Christ is the way. He was "the man". But this means that we ourselves are not yet genuinely human. True humanity still exists in us only in a fragmentary way. We do not find ourselves in the world ready-made. In us there is always a tension between what we are and what we would like to be, between what we have already achieved and what there is still for us to do. In order to be genuine human beings we must always begin anew, always decide afresh to agree with life as human beings.

Ancient philosophy and usage called this constant, almost obstinate endeavour to develop in our being what is vital, beautiful and promising for the future by a much-abused moral term that today is irritating to many, namely "virtue". The significance and magnitude of what is meant by it is experienced by a man only when he becomes aware that his life has not developed as it could have and should have. It is for man to complete his own being. It is for him to ripen, by his own efforts, towards the full realization of the possibilities he contains in himself. If he really tries to do that (that is, if he honestly tries to become a genuine man), then he is approaching what Christ realized: pure humanity, human authenticity fully lived out. After the incarnation of God man needs to do nothing else to find God but to become a human being. More severely expressed (in the language of the Church Fathers): "God has become man in order that man becomes God." I find God in my own humanity. In that man "practises" his humanity (this is the definition of "virtue", after all), he becomes "transparent to God". Dietrich Bonhoeffer said: "God is the beyond in the middle of my life."

But this also means that human authenticity is humanly unattainable. No one is "virtuous", least of all those who consider themselves such. Humanness always exists at a frontier, simply because it is a constant growing into divinity. This means that, in order to become truly human, a man's life must transcend his own limitations and move towards the boundless, a dynamic infinity. The incarnate God draws us out of our littleness, our world of habit. If we are satisfied with what we have already achieved, then we are not as God created us, that is, not men who are moving towards an infinite perfection.

To cultivate this dynamic infiniteness of our existence does not, however, require an enormous effort. God has become our brother, our neighbour. Therefore man can accomplish his movement towards divine perfection in simple straightforward brotherliness, in the humble everyday service of his neighbour. "What you have done for the least of my brethren, you have done for me." That is why the encounter with our neighbour is the opportunity to cultivate human authenticity and thus is the way to God. Thus we have replaced the two questions we asked at the beginning by a third: "How do I find my way to my brother?" If we now put these three questions in a logical order, they give us a statement of the essence of the Gospel of Christ: by finding your way to your brother, you become a true human being and at the same time find God.

Now we have found the Christian logic of our meditations: to find our way through our brother to true humanity precisely in this true humanity to God. Brother—man—God: this will be the basic plan of our thinking. But as far as the actual contents are concerned, we should like to ponder in prayer on the existentially significant virtues—not in unbroken succession, but at least in a logical one—and perhaps also try to practise them a little. Virtue, in the Christian view, is human essentialness that has been achieved through one's own exertions. But just for that reason it is something that is humanly unattainable. To attempt, nevertheless, to reach the unattainable and to receive each success as an undeserved grace is probably the mystery of being a Christian (but also that of friendship and love). The higher the prize, the more it is given. That is why the less the present is deserved, the more it must be earned. It is won precisely in being given freely.

We shall begin our meditations at that point which is the metaphysical root of human unauthenticity, with the life, or rather—so that we do not immediately get caught up in negatives—at the point at which man, in his realized positivity makes divine being speak: with truthfulness.

MEETING GOD IN MAN

1. TRUTHFULNESS

Let us first honestly examine our own lives. They contain moments of honesty, clarity and openness. But this is not our existential situation. Our day-to-day living is largely a lie. We more or less lie our way through life. We all wear masks and constantly avoid what is authentic. The word "lie" is used here not so much in the sense of a conscious falsification of the facts, of an untrue statement that deceives our neighbour, but of a central existential experience, of the untruth of our whole life. Let us try first of all to understand this profound unreality of our life, this shadow over the whole of our existence, so that subsequently the greatness and authenticity of the true man can emerge all the more clearly.

What is a life that is a lie (*Lebenslüge*)? Let us proceed carefully and not involve ourselves, to begin with, in definitions. Let us first look simply at our own lives. Let us attempt to describe the situation in which we are all living.

Our living is largely an avoiding. We do not want to face things, events and men. If we are avoiding something, we are not, it is true, telling a verbal lie. But yet there is a lie in our life. Perhaps we still do not act with secret intentions, we are not denying anything. We are simply avoiding. We pass by when a man is lying in front of us in physical or spiritual distress. We do not bend down beside him. Perhaps we have good reasons for not doing so. To provide a solid foundation for these "good reasons", people even construct systems and open schools of truth. The liar who lies with his full existential power perhaps proclaims the truth with the greatest possible loudness and solemnity. Perhaps he even achieves extraordinary things. But that still does not alter the basic fact that he is ignoring the suffering of others, perhaps even with a smile on his face. An absolute commandment is presented to us, and we avoid it, we "deal" with it, we translate it, we reinterpret it.

Let us take an example. Three friends sit before Job after he and they have sat for seven days, silent with terror. Then the three friends begin to speak. They give the suffering man comfort, advice, but above all instruction. Suddenly God tells them that he is not angry with the weeping and mourning of Job, but with the teachers, exhorters and comforters. They were serious, pious and well-meaning people who talked to him. They spoke "words of gold". But they were still wrong, because they did not help Job, who was so close to blaspheming against God, in any human way. They were not concerned with the suffering of their neighbour, but were concerned with instruction, pastoral work, liturgy and preaching. And this is what enraged God. Their teaching, their lectures were good ones. Everything is right, in fact very right about these exhortations. Three good and wise men are trying here to help someone who is suffering. And yet it is as if they are walking past him because they are not dealing with his suffering. It would have been better for them to have remained silent. Job is quite right to answer them as he does: "I have understanding as well as you" (12. 3). And again: "I have heard many such things . . . I also could speak as you do, if you were in my place; I could join words together against you, and shake my head at you. I could strengthen you with my mouth, and the solace of my lips would assuage your pain" (16. 2; 4–5). And again: "Oh that you would keep silent, and it would be your wisdom!" (13. 5). The three have spoken the truth, but they have not encountered their neighbour in his suffering; and thus they have lied with their life. They have preached "timeless truths" and really wanted to help Job with them. But in fact they have said nothing helpful. They did not bring the man who was suffering before them to the truth, to God. They talked truths which turned into lies. That is why they were not witnesses to truth. These three men wanted basically only to assert their own life, to talk themselves out of the situation. They did not make room in their being for the suffering of their neighbour. Thus they denied being, although they spoke the truth.

We have shown here, by means of an extreme example, what is meant by a life that is a lie, a lie that does not necessarily have to be something falsely spoken. If we try to penetrate this existential dishonesty still further, we discover a further quality (*Eigenschaft*)—we should really say "absence of quality" (*Uneigenschaft*)—namely that of *drifting through life*. This is our attempt to give a name to the profound baseness of existential untruthfulness.

The life of man, however one interprets it, is ultimately a striving for the infinite. This kind of life is difficult to live. Man is too lazy. He refuses to listen to the challenge that is put to him. In this rigidity his life shrivels. He develops habits, rules of life, and this takes the freshness, the spirit out of life, for the profoundest region of the spirit is essentially "superior to habit". Thus life becomes monotonous. We try to dispel this monotony through entertainment and adventures. But it grows gradually into boredom, into a dreariness and hollowness that pervade the whole of life. Man becomes closed in on himself and insensitive to the unexpected, to grace. The drive towards what is great gradually loses its power, as well as the expectation of what makes man "genuine", the hope of beauty, goodness, encounter, friendship and love. The heart's unrest is stilled. A dull condition of desirelessness sets in. We begin to find other people difficult to understand and to reject, and even hate, all that is new. Every encounter disturbs one's habits, it upsets one's routine. Nothing must happen that might disturb, or even shatter, the settled framework within which we drift through life.

It is quite possible that such a man as we have described does well in life and is a "solid" chap. But does he know that man has an abyss in the depths of his being, that the finite contains within it the infinite? This kind of life cannot really give itself to anything because, if it did this, it would completely lose itself. It does not experience this joy of self-sacrifice and the grace-given (grace-bringing) loss of one's individual being, so anxiously guarded, and yet not safe because ultimately it cannot be safeguarded. Thus in a "drift-ing" existence there is a profound—often unacknowledged—antipathy against love, but also against everything that calls for sacrifice. Habits become too strong. Life becomes "solid". But this presumed solidity means only rigidity and ossifica-tion, not the beneficent clarity and crystal hardness of true life.

The whole of life becomes petty. Often we are surprised to find how people who we would expect to be generous, because of their talent, their profession, and their social position, prove, on closer acquaintance, to be petty and small-minded, how often they lack mental and truly human stature. On the other hand, genuine human greatness and also generosity can be revealed in a plain, simple man who is considered to be of hardly any account, when we get near enough to him to experience the radiance of his being. The latter is living, the former is drifting.

The drifting life gradually becomes lazy, mindless and generally "lifeless". Every encounter with true humanity shows it how spiritually powerless it really is. This inner powerlessness makes such men uncertain, although they can often remain calm in the face of deeply shattering experi-ences. Nevertheless they are not equal to the real problems of life.

This fundamental uncertainty slowly becomes anxiety, ex-istential laziness. A man loses his spirit in the real sense: he has lost the courage necessary for true life. In holding on to himself, he has lost himself. That is why this kind of life, even if it seems externally gay and free, has a profound quality of ill-temper about it, a hidden bad mood. The remarkable thing about human life, however, is that it only becomes truly solid by remaining "labile": flexible, sensitive, open to the sur-prising. If man attempts simply to drift, then he is attempting something of which no man is really capable: to be entirely superficial. But the great privilege of man is dissatisfaction and waiting for what is still to come. Whoever stops doing this gives up life itself.

We have tried to outline the existential dishonesty of hu-

man life. We did not speak of a "lie", in the moral sense, but
of a dishonesty of life. This is seen essentially in avoiding and
drifting. Now on the basis of the "hollow mould" of what we
all largely are, let us try to discover what we really ought to
be: human truthfulness. Let us do this by applying the basic
plan of Christian life that we outlined at the beginning ("The
way to our brother leads to true humanity and at the same
time to God also") to the theme of our meditation and thus
let the longing for truthfulness break forth from the depths
of our heart.

Truthfulness towards our brother

Now our language becomes more difficult, even ponderous.
When we spoke previously about existential dishonesty, we
were speaking from our own experience. Now we must speak
of something that we can only surmise, something which we
can only long for. None of us has realized it in his life, not
even fragmentarily. The thing that we want to discuss here is
so simple that human language can express it only in a com-
plicated way. We are concerned here with the "quality of
light" in our life.

It would be very important to speak here also about honesty
of speech towards other men. It consists in the speaker saying
what he really means, sees and understands; that he does not
falsify, abbreviate, change or colour. This is meant, of course,
on condition that the other has the right to be instructed by
us. And yet we must here exclude this very important aspect
of truthfulness—truth of speech has suffered much damage
in our time—or rather accept it as automatic. If someone leads
a developed and critical Christian life, is able to conquer his
shyness and embarrassment and still possesses the necessary
control of language, he will himself discover how one can and
must speak the truth in our strangely confused world.

We are concerned here, however, with a much more important thing, namely the question of what a life looks like
that not only speaks the truth, but also does it, that is a life in
which truth "blazes up", becoming immediate experience.

Let us again proceed cautiously and outline, first simply phenomenologically, the image of a life that "does" the truth. What does such a "luminous" life look like? Our description must necessarily be subjective. We shall simply try first to say what we have experienced or only guessed in our encounter with men whose life is luminous. Thus we must not outline a system, but must string together loosely, at first glance, qualities that do not automatically belong together. In this way we shall obtain a picture, and not a definition, of truth towards our brother.

Truly honest men have the capacity, which has practically become part of their nature, of arousing love and friendship. Why? That is very hard to say and still more difficult to describe. Perhaps because they are wholly "open to receive". Without any set intention they receive our being into themselves; they want nothing from us; they do not try to get anything out of us; they do not want to bind anyone to them. The human soul simply enjoys being with such men, although they are generally very quiet, even taciturn, and like being by themselves. They radiate a joy that speaks of an inner strength. This strength makes them somehow fearless. This quality is necessary if a man opens his soul without reservations to other men. The heart of this kind of "existentially honest" life is withdrawn from the influence of what is terrible in the mortal and in man. This is a sign of special election. It is seen above all in the fact that such men do not resent offences, or even do not have to pardon offences. One never has the impression with them that they were consciously pardoning the offender. They possess a quiet innocence. They never took the offence as such, indeed never even saw it as such. This is that selflessness of which we have already spoken: in such men there is room for the human "thou", room in which the other man can achieve free existence.

Often such men of total honesty leave no visible trace behind them in the world. They often disappear from it with their luminousness as if they had never existed. Quite simply and quietly they pass into the greater beyond. But they work on, in the conscience of those they have met in life, as a spiritual power. They judge us through their truthfulness, precisely by not condemning us. True, they clearly differentiate what is right and what is wrong. They do not agree when it is impossible, but they do not judge, often they go away simply silent. But precisely in this there is a true judgment, something which cannot take place, or only seldom, in the lawcourts of our world. They judge us by holding fast to what they have seen, to the truth, but without emphasizing it in any way or forcing themselves upon us. They lack that objectionable quality of pretending to know better in everything.

This quality of not emphasizing themselves in any way could also be described as an essential chastity. Such men are committed with their whole being to the ultimate reality, that is holiness. They often live with a "holy carelessness". Often they have no inner relation to money, they sometimes give everything away and have themselves nothing left on which to live. Their life is essentially without care. They realize the morals of Christ, often without knowing much about him: "Take no care for the morrow." Not everyone can live in this way. But there must be such men among us, in order that life remains alive.

The truthful man combines with the quality of not judging an existential simplicity and transparency. Such men are truthful in the sense that they sometimes feel the inner urge to speak the truth, to have to go to another person and say to him, you are playing a role before the world and yourself; stop it. It suddenly comes over them, like an illumination: I must tell this man the truth, otherwise no one will. But a special strength flows from such men. If they think about it afterwards, they do not know themselves how they could dare to speak the whole truth. There is fear, both in the speaker and in the man he speaks to, a fear of the holy. At the same time there is joy, even rejoicing: being shines out in its pure radiance. Someone has dared to speak the truth. Something firm and unshakable has come into being, something that shines and burns and yet again is love and selflessness.

But we must remember how vulnerable such a being is. It is an unbearable thing to be the living conscience of others.

No man can stand that for a long time. That is why precisely the truthful man is endangered. He stands in the world as an ambassador of truth. But the mission is also a trial. All that we have tried to describe hitherto, this fearlessness, this chastity, this freedom from care contain the possibility of a collapse. Only he can fall who stands on an eminence. Discouragement, insecurity and temptation overcome him. He asks: did I really speak the truth that heals? Was I not too hard? Was I not too self-righteous? And very probably he was.

Truthfulness towards one's own being

The apostle Paul, who was sometimes able to look amazingly deeply into the human heart, exhorted his friends in Ephesus to speak the truth in love. The Greek expression is almost untranslatable: "aletheúein en agápe" (Eph. 4. 15); which means, more or less, "truth oneself out—*sich auswahrheiten*—(say, do and be the truth), but in love".

We are tempted all too often to say things at the wrong moment, when we injure others by the truth, or even do them harm. Thus truthfulness towards one's brother must be supported by tact and goodness. We cannot use truthfulness like a stick. In this continual self-examination, which must be constantly undertaken afresh, inner truth emerges, to which we can give no other name but humility. Precisely to the extent that a man tries to "be truth" for others, he recognizes that he himself is not equal to the demands that he makes—apparently only for others. Through this he learns modesty. He starts to be patient with himself and others and lets the fruit of truth ripen quietly. This gives strength to his life: only strong men can practise living patience, that is support the tension within them between what they would like to have, and what they really have; between what they ought to do, and what they are actually able to do; between what they want to be and what they really are. From this inner tension there grows patience with others, which is not a cowardly giving in, but a genuine forbearance and kindness.

Is not such a life an almost impossible burden: to have to

speak the truth and not to be it? This is the deepest experience of a person who is trying to be truth for others. He must be truth, but cannot be. Both facts exist, irreducibly. What takes place in a man who has the experience that he is truth, although he is not? He experiences God. Something shattering takes place in the man who is making himself truth: the "wholly other" breaks into the world, that which cannot be achieved and created by human power. He has to give, with empty hands. The incredible thing is that he really can do it. This is no proof of God. But if someone has once experienced this, he cannot help believing in God. From his own impotence, which suddenly—as from an inner drive—turns into power, without his deserving it, he recognizes with certainty God himself. Thus there comes into being in the world:

Truthfulness from God

If a person can support this tension of his life for long enough, he will see absolute being shine out in the world: the creature standing radiant in the light of the infinite. Perhaps we can best see this transformation of humanity into the transparency of the absolute in the accounts of the risen Christ. A radical transformation of being is indicated there. A boundlessness of space, time, power and light opens up before us. This man—one at least—has become the glory, the intensity of reality, the shining flame of essential being. To get an idea of this we need only read the opening vision of the Secret Revelation (Apocalypse) or the account of the transformation (transfiguration) of Christ on Mount Tabor. Perhaps we should meditate here on all the accounts of the appearances of the risen Christ in order to grasp, at least in part, what it means to say that a man has become wholly transparent to the absolute. Instead of that, let us try to show how the apostles experienced Christ, who is *the* truth, and how they became his witnesses, that is how they began to radiate the truth of Christ through the world. In the encounter with the incarnate God they become first, as the Epistle to the Ephesians says, men with "the eyes of (their) hearts

enlightened" (Eph. 1. 18). Living with Christ, even in quite
mundane situations, they experienced what it is when the
glory of God lights up a human face (2 Cor. 4. 6).

At first this experience put them in a state of wonderment.
The gospels speak of this spiritual condition, which all men
experience who receive the truth from God, in the form of
puzzling stories, of "miracles". Here we cannot even begin to
outline a theology of miracles, but only point out *en passant*
that Christ was really *the* miracle. Something completely new
was suddenly among us: "Jesus, the saviour is here!" Christ
was the real and decisive miracle, the miracle of miracles;
Christ, who made the apostles men who were lost in wonder
once and for all. The miracles were mere external alarm
signals of this wonderment that comes upon any man when
Christ, in whatever form, comes close to him.

This wonderment increased in the apostles to the point of
amazement. They took a risk when they became involved
with this "radiant man", who struck them in the heart of
their anxious being. One can follow the traces of this amazement in all the writings of the New Testament. One cannot
mess about with this man. He seeks us; his secret comes upon
us. He comes right up to us and asks: "Brother, how is your
heart?" God once called similarly: "Adam, where are you?"
It is no longer an unattached, unbinding statement about
truth that stands before this horrified man, but a person.

This is the basic amazement: God appears in a man who
seeks me out, who commits me to an inner truth, who tries
me. This involves testing. Man must constantly test himself
to see how he stands in relation to this incarnate truth, truth
become man. And Christ makes the apostles go through this
experience. With his own life he brings them into a great
danger. This is strangely woven out of a lonely struggle, out
of inner doubt, out of the risk of faith, out of temptation,
and out of the "nevertheless" of hope. Paul asks of all Christians the same painful self-testing: "Examine yourselves, to
see whether you are holding to your faith. Test yourselves. Do
you not realize that Jesus Christ is in you? Unless indeed
you fail to meet the test" (2 Cor. 13. 5).

When the test has been met—again we could pursue this process, in all its details, through the whole Gospel—that commitment comes about that makes these men witnesses of the truth: a tendency of our thinking, sensibility, feeling and of our whole life. It is impossible now not to follow the absolute truth that shines forth in Christ. Nothing counts any longer, no bond, no system of thought, no position of power, no friendship, not even love. Only Christ is there. In this way man becomes a child of light: "Once you were darkness, but now you are light in the Lord; walk as children of light" (Eph. 5. 8). We acquire a "burning heart": the Emmaus disciples invented this phrase to describe their Easter experience. "Did not our hearts burn within us while he talked to us on the road . . . ?" (Luke 24. 32).

And it is the burning heart that is the testimony of Christ in the world. We must transform ourselves into light. From now on there is no way out; we are eternally pledged to be burning. An almost intolerable task. The Christian should plunge himself in this imperious "I desire" that the departing Lord spoke over us on the threshold and in which he sought to make us witnesses and sharers of his radiance, his glory. "Father, I desire that they also, whom thou hast given me, may be with me where I am, to behold my glory which thou hast given me in thy love for me before the foundation of the world" (John 17. 24).

Man receives as grace the power to be light: it comes upon, it befalls him. The "wondering", "amazed" and "tested" life is filled with fire. This is the inner meaning of that event of which the Acts of the Apostles stammeringly speaks: "Suddenly a sound came from heaven like the rush of a mighty wind, and it filled all the house where they were sitting. And there appeared to them tongues as of fire distributed and resting on each one of them" (2. 2–3). These flashes of glory have the form of "tongues": the illuminated man must speak. He must stand up and go out into a world of darkness, in order to bear witness to the truth that is Christ.

The greatness of what this means is seen in the most vivid way in the figure of the first martyr, Stephen: this young man filled with the spirit is representative of the truth. He is the bearer of the Spirit that "comes from above", but is inescapably at the mercy of the power that "comes from below". Suddenly the martyr sees reality: "I see the heavens opened, and the Son of man standing at the right hand of God." (Let us note the difference: the Son of man "stands" and does not "sit", as in Mark 16. 19). And testimony, a revelation, is given in his face: "And gazing at him, all who sat in the council saw that his face was like the face of an angel" (Acts 6. 15). An angelic face, that is a face that, in the midst of temporal tribulation, is wholly reshaped by the eternal mode of being. . . . The angelic radiance of his face is the victory of the first martyr and the symbol of the power of the Christian which is superior to the world. A radiant victory, but "radiant in the abyss of death" (Eugen Biser, *Das Licht des Lammes*).

This power from above—and this is the last point in our description of how the apostles experienced the truth of Christ, with its attendant suffering—gives to the apostles a holy fearlessness. They are able and allowed to proclaim the truth to all men, because it is not "their" truth; because they are not acting on their own impulse. For this reason—but only for this—they have the right to "free language", a holy freedom of speech, an omnipotence of the word (*parrhesia*).

John, especially, had the shattering experience, which he also expressed, that from now on it is possible to speak freely; above all to God. "Beloved, if our hearts do not condemn us, we have confidence (to speak—*parrhesia*) before God; and we receive from him whatever we ask" (1 John 3. 21–22). And again: "This is the confidence (*parrhesia*) which we have in him, that if we ask anything according to his will he hears us. And if we know that he hears us in whatever we ask, we know that we have obtained the requests made of him" (1 John 5. 14–15).

However, we find the most significant interpretation, for us, of this fearlessness in Paul. The free stating of the truth becomes in him the essential task of the Christian: it is the radiance of the glory of the absolute in the world. The Christian becomes part of the openness of God to the world. In

the Second Letter to the Corinthians, Paul gives an interpretation of the fearlessness of the Christian in testifying to
the truth (we should read carefully the text of 2 Cor. 3. 12–
4. 6): "We all, with unveiled face, beholding the glory of the
Lord, are being changed into his likeness from one degree of
glory to another; for this comes from the Lord who is the
Spirit" (3. 18). An incomprehensible event: man, doubting,
inwardly torn, discontented and insecure is surrounded by
radiant glory and becomes a Christ for his fellow men, a likeness of Christ. "By the open statement of the truth we would
commend ourselves to every man's conscience in the sight of
God" (4. 2–3). "For what we preach is not ourselves, but
Jesus Christ as Lord." "The light of the knowledge of the
glory of God in the face of Christ" (4. 5–6). But this always
in the awareness that "we have this treasure in earthen ves-
sels, to show that the transcendent power belongs to God
and not to us. We are afflicted in every way, but not crushed;
perplexed, but not driven to despair; persecuted, but not forsaken; struck down, but not destroyed" (4. 7–10). In an afflicted, perplexed, persecuted and struck-down man the rich
and radiant truth breaks through. This is expressed in a painful "yet", in the "nevertheless" of not being crushed, not
being driven to despair, not feeling oneself forsaken, not letting oneself be destroyed.

Thus, in a painful and often undramatic way, the world is
made solid and strengthened—by God. We understand the
secret meaning of Christ's words: "Was it not necessary that
the Christ should suffer these things and enter into his glory?"
(Luke 24. 26). To live in such a way, as a witness of the
truth that flows from God, as a witness of Christ, is an un-
losable joy, but a joy that is born from suffering. "You have
sorrow now, but I will see you again and your hearts will
rejoice, and no one will take your joy from you. In that day
you will ask nothing of me" (John 16. 22–23).

2. RESPECT

In our second section, let us now penetrate further into this attitude of life which is given by God, is open to one's brother, and creates human reality, an attitude that—despite the fact that the word is hackneyed, indeed precisely because it is hackneyed, since we want to restore to the word its full value—we have called virtue. A man achieves his fullest relationship with God by constantly practising an attitude of openness towards his brother. In our first section we have already pointed out that human truthfulness is possible only in an attitude of thoughtfulness that is sensitive to the unique nature of others. We should now like to develop our ideas in this direction a little further.

Let us again first look at the negative side. It is easier to speak of it, because it comes from our own experience. The dominant quality in our heart is contempt, dislike. We could even put it more harshly and call it cruelty. The more one looks into one's own life, the more one becomes aware how often and how many people one has inwardly rejected, almost as an instinctive reaction.

Sometimes this painful experience of our own hardness of heart can increase to the point that we are tempted. We ask: Why am I such that I offend and hurt my best friends? Did God create me like this? If God exists and if he is an all-kind and all-powerful being, how can he allow men to hate one another, that they do harm to one another, that the world is full of frightful horrors before which we must constantly shut our eyes and our heart, because otherwise we could not go on living? Why am I so petty, so inwardly ugly, so loveless and sometimes so cruel? Is there such a thing as a God? If he really existed, I could not have so many terrible things within me. This idea is very important, because, if we reverse it, it makes us aware of our true Christian task.

If we ourselves are bad and cruel towards others, then they are tempted, then for them there is no God. The relation of their life to the absolute is shattered by our life. Every mean thing that we do to another person proves to him that there is no God. Of course there is so much that is lovable and beautiful, so much radiance in our world that it is possible to sense God's existence in it with every fibre of one's being. And yet, we all have the experience that the loss of a single person can lead us to complete loneliness; a single being is missing, a single smile, and everything is barren and empty.

On the other hand, however, it can also happen that, if we withdraw ourselves from a single person, if we reject him or are even cruel to him, we can make the whole world abhorrent to him. God wants to enter the world in us and through us, he wants to be kind through us. He has taken this extraordinary risk. This is the task that is involved in being a Christian: to be God's goodness, so that men can recognize that goodness and benevolence exist, that, "despite everything", being is good. If we are Christians, we must prove to others that tomorrow will be a better day. In this they experience God: total benevolence and infinite love. There are proofs of God that refute unbelief with logical impeccability. But in the grave crises of human existence they mean nothing, or very little. In such times there must be a man whose life is at least a sign that humanity is respected and honoured, that it is taken up into an unconditional friendship, that is, that he really exists who makes all possible: God.

That is why, in an age in which the face of God is obscured, it is so important that we destroy the contempt in our hearts, so that the whole sympathy with being, which slumbers within us, can break forth, the total affirmation of others, and thus our life become a "proof of God" for them. But this can happen only if first we discover the basis of our contempt. In as much as we are able to grasp it at all, it is fourfold.

In the depth of all our actions we will discover a self-seeking quality. We are thinking here not so much of the crude forms of human egoism, which destroys the life of others, only in order to obtain advantages for oneself, that seeks to be victorious over others simply for the sake of victory. We are thinking here rather of that turning back to ourselves which is very difficult to describe, but is a quality that runs through, and indeed overgrows, our whole life. Only occasionally is man able to get away from this existential turning back on himself. Only in the great enthusiasm of friendship and love does he succeed—occasionally—to be purely there for others. For the most part, however, we remain a victim to ourselves, even in actions which externally appear so unselfish. We are held captive by a subtle self-reflection. It is terrifying to see how men who strove for the purest human integrity, the saints, constantly struggled against this self-seeking which permeated their whole being and yet constantly succumbed to it. In our unconscious self-assertion we daily annihilate men who irritate us. Our self-seeking is often hidden under a mask of little nervous habits, moral indignation, self-righteousness, of tiny humiliations to which we subject others.

Behind this, and perhaps still deeper, there is hidden a strange incapacity of man to love. In his heart he constantly betrays those whom he really loves most. True, there are great, intense "spiritual" moments in the life of man, in which he attains the summit of self-immolation. Afterwards he possibly does nothing for the rest of his life but take back all that he had given in this moment of spiritual bravery and love. With unimaginable energy and tough endurance man must climb up the hill, the difficult slope of his own incapacity to love, if he desires to realize only a small part of the sacrifice that is asked of him. Man cannot really love. At the end we have nothing, not our happiness, nor even our unhappiness. Our life is a strange and painful leave-taking from those whom we want to love, in fact it is a leave-taking from our love itself. We are men who were sent into the adventure of love, as it were, without weapons. Every attempt at love divides our heart. Time is too short. We learn true devotion always too late, always afterwards. In our life it is always too late. Too late we notice the suffering of human beings whom we might have helped; too late we realize that a friendship was offered to us; too late we see that someone really loved us.

An honest analysis of our own incapacity to love finds at the base of our own actions something like a profound, as it were, inborn dislike. This dislike is a veiled denial of the being of others, that is, hatred. Our dislike is able to hide itself; it is often repressed into the unconscious and emerges only in other forms in our consciousness, as antipathy, indifference, irritability. Who could describe and investigate this human dislike? Even our liking for others is often based on dislike: a superficial relation of love or friendship conceals a will to destroy. We bind someone else to us in order to be able to torture him the better.

All this is expressed and concentrated in our life as rejection. We harden our hearts because we fear the strenuousness of love. In us there lurks the urge to enslave our fellow man, to appropriate him like a thing. What we call love is often nothing but an intolerant will to have complete possession of another person. Through this the other person becomes a mere thing. But a thing does not satisfy our love; so our love changes into hate, into a desire to destroy the "object" of love which has so disappointed us, in order to prove at least that we have become the "possessor". How often is our love only a means to self-assertion! We no longer listen to the cry, to the pleading of our fellow man. When we reject a man who desperately begs to be liked by us, we hand him over to destruction, in fact we destroy him, in so far as it lies in our power, by our refusal.

If we believe in God, we must create some sort of order in our life, which—we must be honest and admit it—mostly consists of selfishness, incapacity to love, dislike and rejection. And this order is called respect. Let us now again allow the ultimate desire of our heart to speak, even if men tell us we are dreamers who chase after the impossible and make ourselves ridiculous. It is only what is humanly unattainable that is worthy of being attained. We all long for an order in which man can exist truly as a person, as a loved and lovable centre of affirmation.

The world must be judged. The word "judged" arouses in us an unpleasant feeling; but the more we see through the world, its motives, its striving for power and self-assertion, the more we look into our own heart, the more we become aware that we do not live in a world that is right.[1] The world only becomes right when the good is also beautiful, the true also good, and being also luminous. This world does not yet exist, as we know from our own life. It must be created by us, though it is a gift we receive. What would this right world be like? It would be a world in which a man who is good would also be happy, in which the desire of the heart would also be revealed as action, in which the pure would always be beautiful, in which the light of the good man would also be fulfilled in a rich and great way. And, *vice versa*, a world in which a mean mind would make a man ugly, injustice would also bring unhappiness, guilt would always be avenged on the guilty one—and only on him, never on an innocent victim. In reality things are quite different. The exertion to create a right world is called the virtue of respect. In it the world emerges in its right form. Let us now speak of this.

Respect for one's brother

Respect for a person is really reverence. The German word for this is *Ehrfurcht*—a strange word combined of "fear" (*Furcht*) and "honour" (*Ehre*). Fear which shows honour. It is a holy respect for what is great in the other person. In it a man renounces the possession of the other person, the using of him for his own purposes. He takes his hands away, instead of grabbing. A true humanity is created only where a man steps back, where he does not force himself forward, does not snatch at things; in this way a free space is created in the world in which the other person can flourish in his

[1] There is here an untranslatable play on the German words "richten", "to judge" and "richtig", "right"—Trans.

own nature, dignity and beauty. When a friendship collapses or a marriage coarsens, Romano Guardini suggests that whoever is concerned should ask himself whether he has not failed in respect, whether he has not treated the other person like a piece of furniture.

We have all met men who were able to recognize true greatness. To recognize greatness is the basic condition of respect. A man must be able to say: He is great, I am not. But it is good that greatness exists in the world, even if it is not in me, but in the other. Greatness should be affirmed, because it exists, because it is beautiful. It is vitally necessary to acknowledge it, even if our own life shrinks before it. It is a good thing that the other has been able to do this.

The revered man, however, is able to recognize greatness even in the small man, indeed, precisely in him, even in the despised and unworthy man, but above all in the defenceless man, who is incapable of asserting himself. The revered man feels himself called to be respectful precisely to the defenceless. It comes automatically to him to help a child or weak man; he stops before fate and is touched by it. If a man wants the most precious thing he can out of life, which lasts so few years, years that so quickly pass, then he must know that the real meaning of his existence does not consist in enjoying himself and his power, but in realizing what advances life; that wherever life appears, he must give it space and help it to grow.

This greatness which appears in smallness is made clear by a mysterious statement in Scripture: "Whosoever humbles himself like this child, he is the greatest in the kingdom of heaven" (Matt. 18. 4). This greatness of smallness is hidden in mystery. It is a triple mystery. First, behind the humble there are the omnipresent, most powerful beings in the world, the angels: "See that you do not despise one of these little ones; for I tell you that in heaven their angels always behold the face of my Father who is in heaven" (Matt. 18. 10). Secondly and thirdly: The greatness of the small appears even more profoundly and impressively in the fact that in smallness the incarnate God and, through him, the almighty Father become themselves directly present: "Whoever receives one such child in my name receives me; and whoever receives me, receives not me but him who sent me" (Mark 9. 37). Three tremendous statements that we should ponder deeply. Helplessness and defencelessness are something so holy that they are directly under the protection of the eternal beings of creation and of the Trinity. All truly great men protect children, the defenceless, the dispossessed and the unfortunate; they always believe in their dignity and their good will; they approach them with confidence, without pedagogical intentions, quite naturally. This does them good, it makes them free, it makes it possible for the many people who have to live together in the narrow space of our world to be able to do it without injuring one another.

A man who does honour to all, with plain, unpushing courtesy and simple readiness to help, always and everywhere conquers that in his own being which threatens to strangle life. This quality that threatens to strangle life is something to which it is very difficult to give a name. Perhaps the most suitable description would be "not meaning well towards life". It consists of the desire to dominate and of sulkiness and envy. The positive quality that shines out from a man who means well towards life is tolerance, well-wishing, goodness. Wherever such a man encounters life, his first impulse is not to mistrust and criticize, but to respect, to be tolerant, and to help to grow.

We have some sense here of how dangerous it is for us to radiate this goodness in the world. The good man always experiences suffering as well. But suffering seeks to be understood; it asks for help and sympathy. But this is tiring, it calls for an effort, which perhaps only consists in finding at this moment for this man those words that alleviate his immediate distress. Great patience is also necessary to listen to the complaint of a man and to understand it in its unique quality. Sometimes one already knows by heart what they will say to us. Human suffering is often so banal that one has

to restrain oneself with all one's strength from brutally revealing how ordinary and hackneyed it is. Yet for the suf-
ferer it is his unique suffering. The man who has respect must
be ready to listen again and again in patience to the same
sad story and not to say to the other person, who is perhaps
taking himself too seriously: You are boring with your eternal
complaining. Often simply a quiet inner smile about the
strangeness of human life is a help, a smile that makes us able
once more to be kind and understanding, despite everything,
towards the suffering of the other. For this one needs inner
peace and serenity. This quiet respect nourishes life. It gives
birth to kindness and understanding.

Understanding means primarily that man develops a sensitivity of feeling and a capacity for sympathy which bridges
the strangeness between men. In this way a common benevolence is born. But it is acquired only through experience,
experience from which one really learns: one's eye becomes
gradually more perceptive, one's sensitivity more refined, and
one's adaptability greater. This again is only possible if man
can free himself from his instinctive attitude of sympathy
or antipathy and tries to accept the other person as he is; if
he no longer divides the world into people who are attractive
and unattractive, but says to every being: You have a right to
be as you are.

This quiet, kind and understanding attitude towards other
beings is at the same time humility. It endeavours above all
not to make life worse than it already is. The more familiar
one is with the world of the heart, the more profoundly one
realizes that every bad word that one speaks poisons the air
for the whole of humanity; that every lie and every violent
action brings even greater confusion into the life of our neigh-
bours. The man who is filled with respect for other life prays:
Lord, I have done many bad things in your beautiful world;
I must bear with patience what the others are and what I
myself am; give it to me that I can do something so that life
becomes a little better where you have placed me.

This kind of humility endeavours to realize the firm command of Christ: "Judge not" (Matt. 7. 1). We can see that most of the judgments that one man makes about another are basically nothing but self-assertion: you are pleasant to me, he is not; I can use you, I cannot use him. Thus to the man who is kindly disposed towards life there is gradually revealed the holiness of being. The eye of such a man discovers in us what we are not yet, but should become, he arouses in us the possibilities and hopes that lie in us. In this way we learn that we ourselves, despite our ordinariness and smallness, are truly great, and we become aware of our own holiness.

Respect for one's own existence

If we try to accept our own life as holy, that is, as inviolable and calling for reverence, a liberation takes place. Primarily, remarkably enough, a liberation of our own self. We see that the real thing, what is truly worthy of respect in our own life is not our self, but that which shines behind it: the mysterious otherness. A man who respects himself in all honesty does not respect his self. Who am I, that I, with my pride, my absurdity, my tired failures, could still respect myself? And yet I discover that there is a point in me at which I touch the absolute, about which I can say nothing further; that I am moving into the infinite, into something that transcends anything that I could say about it; that I am infinitely more, know infinitely more, conceive and long for infinitely more than I can ever realize; that this infinite and inexpressible realm is closer to me than my own self; hence that, from the start, I am not myself; that I cannot say anything about a similarity between this, the essential part of my existence and myself that is not cancelled out by a dissimilarity that is, as it were, mortal and, for that very reason, life-giving. I am worthy of reverence precisely for what I am not and what nevertheless is part of my own existence. I must feel respect for precisely this holy part of me. I must accept myself: my situation in life, my environment, my friends, my failures, my historical epoch, my outer and inner fate, the direction of my life, my character, my terrifying mediocrity, and my despair. And in this I affirm the other, inexpressible, the absolute and ultimate. To be truly human is to experience, within one's final limitation, an openness to the infinite and to live it out in a way that is credible to others. One becomes one's self in liberating oneself from oneself.

This liberation from oneself, however, involves at the same time a distancing of oneself from the world. By the world we mean here our impulses, our prejudices, our nervous reflexes. The essential part of human existence transcends all that. A man must not be equated with himself, his habits, prejudices and predecisions, with the pull of ordinary everyday life, with the positions that he has occupied. True humanity consists of being aware of the surprising, the new; thus it consists in an openness and a remaining open of the human being to an unsuspected perfection. If a man really seeks to be man, he must be able to say no to the meanness of his own life and world. He must live his way into the boundless. He must never be satisfied with himself, his joys, his views and convictions, the cosy God that he has made for himself. Thus a man acquires a holy carefreeness, a boldness of life, a readiness to listen to the voice of what is still greater. What good is it to us if we only remain ourselves and the world only remains the world, if less does not become more?

Respect for oneself, therefore, means an openness to the absolute that dwells within us. This kind of life—away from oneself and away from the smallness of the world, that is, a life of total respect—is certainly a lot to ask. If one wants to become a man, however, something is asked of one, courage is demanded to become truly human.[2] It is very difficult for us men to accept the life of others and our own life. But this is precisely what God wants of us. That is why human

[2] There is here an untranslatable play on words: the German word "zumuten", "to expect something of someone", contains the root "Mut", meaning, in earlier German, "mind", and today, "courage". —Trans.

life cannot really be coped with on the human level. Respect for one's brother and for oneself presumes, therefore, respect on a higher level: the respect of God.

The respect of God

This includes two things, according to the objective and the subjective meaning of the expression.

Man's respect for God. This too must be practised. A special exertion, namely practice in prayer, is necessary in order to become familiar with God, to enjoy having to do with him. It must be worked at, faithfully and with self-discipline; again and again, always anew. Man must take time for prayer; then there comes, as an undeserved grace, God's nearness to him. An essential part of what this labour achieves is that man becomes completely open to the absolute, that is, that he does not seek to obtain personal advantages from God, only the one thing: to open himself, to give himself, without any other aim.

Precisely to the extent to which a man gives himself to this desireless existence in harmony with the absolute, there grows in him his true humanity. Then man is simply there, without pressing himself forward in any way. The external self is somehow extinguished, and reality shines through human existence. This essential detachment of man from himself in the face of the absolute is called adoration. God alone is good; he alone is worthy of adoration, he alone is great. In adoration man bows before the absolute. Not just deeply, but absolutely deeply. Not only to that inner point which is still part of one's own inner life, but beyond that, to the deepest and most essential level. This kind of adoration affects us like a pure light, clear air. From adoration there comes an unshakable trust, the awareness that, despite all difficulties and shattering experiences, despite all the powers that may stand against us (even in spite of our own self), that we are safe and cared for in God's almighty power.

It should surprise us that in Christian prayer so much petition, thanks and sometimes also praise is in the foreground, and that adoration, this essential act of relating ourselves to the absolute, hardly appears. Adoration is not easy today; hence it must be practised with special effort. We are daily faced with so many impressions, demands and duty that we are constantly in danger of forgetting adoration, of simply no longer being able to gather ourselves towards the absolute central point of the significance of being, of no longer standing before it in pure desirelessness, saying nothing, silent, at most expressing the essential thing of our existence: Thou. The everyday bustle of our world has, as it were, pushed God out, it has buried him. We must fight our way free again to be capable of living adoration. Without that we can have no respect for either our brothers or for ourselves. But how does God want to be adored?

God's respect for men. The absolute God has made adoration easy for us by laying aside his intangibility in Christ. This is the mystery of the incarnation: God stands in our midst, unprotected, vulnerable to word and deed; in this way he leads us out of the prison of our own narrowness. Through him the intangible became tangible, the incomprehensible comprehensible. God behaves with such graciousness towards us that he comes to meet us on every path.

The holy graciousness of God is already seen in the fact that he has created us. We can conceive God's creative act only in terms of respect. In Scripture we read: "God said let it be and it was." He created us through a still, quiet word. He *spoke*, quite quietly, the world, life and humanity, in the effortlessness of his omnipotence. Reserve is the actual deed of creation. When he creates, God does not shout at us, he does not set to energetically but he leaves room for being, he withdraws, as it were, his omnipotence, his being that fills everything, in order that we are able to exist at all. The act of creation is an infinitely delicate and quiet touch, a respect that solidifies into being.

This delicacy of God that is called creation became—if one may say so—even more tender, more reserved and more mild in Christ. In Christ God honoured the whole of humanity and hence us all. "Behold, I stand at the door and knock"

(Rev. 3. 20). The power of Christ was quite quiet: "He will not wrangle or cry aloud" (Matt. 12. 19). But he who said this of himself was the man who, as we must prayerfully remember, has been given "all authority in heaven and on earth" (Matt. 28. 18) and who could have broken everything with a rod of iron, "as when earthen pots are broken in pieces" (Rev. 2. 27). He has never fought against others, never humiliated another man. His being was filled by a cosmic respect towards the whole of creation, it was a loving embrace of life, as it came into being and was exposed and threatened, a unique gesture of thoughtful caring. An unprominent sentence from St Mark's gospel gives us profound insight into the inner nature of Christ: "And he was in the wilderness forty days . . . with the wild beasts" (1. 13). The kingdom of peace, of which mankind had always dreamt, had come into the world with him.

Job in his sufferings had a sense of this incarnate tenderness of God: "At destruction and famine you shall laugh, and shall not fear the beasts of the earth. For you shall be in league with the stones of the field" (5. 22–23). Isaiah put it even more strongly: "Be glad and rejoice forever in that which I create. . . . Before they call I will answer, while they are yet speaking I will hear" (65. 18; 24).

We should here recall especially how Christ defended sinners before the just (Luke 5. 31; 15. 1–7; 18. 9–14); the defenceless against the powerful (Mark 10. 14), Mary before Martha and before Judas (Luke 10. 41 and John 12. 7). In Christ there appeared among us a God who refuses to do harm to anything. This made him "the Author of life" (Acts 3. 15). He promised us that we will be satisfied, that we will one day be able to laugh with true joy, that we will inherit the kingdom, the kingdom that lasts for ever. How little do we understand of this reserve of God. His words to Peter are meant for us all: "Put your sword into its sheath" (John 18. 11).

We all have within us a contempt that seems to be inborn, and thus we obscure the face of God in the world. This contempt is made up of selfishness, the incapacity to love, dislike and rejection. We become truly human only by recognizing greatness in others, and above all in the small and helpless; by working ourselves towards life; by exercising patience, seeking to understand others and judging no one. This makes us free to be truly human, it detaches us from ourselves and distances us from the dreariness of our everyday world. We become free to adore, to be there, desireless, in the presence of the absolute. This is so difficult that God himself "had to" become man, so that we should see how it is possible to live in our world this life of tender, quiet, mild desirelessness that is respect. True humanity is possible only from Christ. And, *vice versa*, where there is true humanity, Christ is also. We have considered two virtues, two ways of working to become truly human: truthfulness and respect. Through these attitudes a new dimension of being comes into the world, selflessness. It expresses one of the most fundamental human experiences: we receive life only by fostering life. Still more profoundly: it is only in giving away that we receive a gift. This experience opens up for us new horizons. Still more is asked of us. It is not enough to practise truthfulness and respect in our world. If we want to become selfless, we cannot simply remain selfless. We must give out of ourselves still more, we must squander ourselves. We should become still more one with our brother and in this grow still more towards true humanity, and in this come still nearer to God. Our selflessness is to show itself as service. On this we shall speak in the next two sections.

3. REVERENCE

In our third section we shall go a little more deeply into what we have discussed. We have seen the way in which honestly-lived truthfulness and respect gathers our being ever more to a relation with the Thou, with our brother, how it becomes "selfless". In selflessness man experiences more fully that being is holy and to be revered. This gives him courage for life, courage for self-sacrifice and service. Not some woolly attitude, but a call to give oneself to life in joy and in happy goodwill. Because we have experienced the sacredness of being, we want to protect it by active devotion, especially wherever this being is threatened. We place ourselves in the service of life.

But this can happen only if we revere life, honour it, help it to become more beautiful and more alive. In this way life becomes "intense". We again find pleasure in life, in happiness but, above all, in the joy of others. We begin to help others so that they again can find their way in life, that they can free themselves from all that blocks the path to happiness for them. We promise them more life, we confirm their right and their duty to live and to unfold; we arouse in them a holy enthusiasm for happiness. In this way life becomes vital and easy; we restore it again to honour and help it to grow; we create a fuller life in others, a more concentrated reality. We "honour" a being by crediting him with more being than the external appearance shows, that is, by discovering something greater, higher and more worthwhile in him than meets the eye and helping this to develop. For this a large measure of high-mindedness is necessary: a feeling for high things that has become part of one's mentality.

In order, however, to be able to show life this reverence, to increase what is beautiful in it and gives joy, man must first himself strive to experience the beauty and holiness of being. Do we do that? Do we feel enthusiasm for life? We must again, I am afraid, begin with a negative description.

Generally life appears to us dull and heavy. Sometimes we are really fed up with it. What filled us with enthusiasm years ago and roused us to love, suddenly appears to be of no interest or even a burden. We drag out our life. Life does not mean anything to us any more, it no longer attracts us; we endure it, we manage somehow. Even this endurance of life is an effort. Everything is colourless and boring. We no longer have any real interest in what we are doing. We express this great disappointment at life in bad moods, unkind judgments, in facial expressions of distaste. We still do what we have to. We support our fate, but we become more and more fed up. The joy goes out of life. We seek pleasure in order to escape from still worse boredom. We complain (and that is a bad sign) of being crushed by work and by our cares. Everything becomes banal and hackneyed. We no longer find real joy in anything. We become incapable of enjoying the good in life.

What have we really achieved? Have we really done anything? The profession that we embraced at first with such enthusiasm, even plunging into it, gradually becomes more tedious, even without meaning, a treadmill of the daily round. Boring work, useless and senseless things. How can we still have pleasure in things that we have so often betrayed?

The people around us also become boring. We have said everything to them that was of any interest; we cannot say anything to them that has real reality; and we no longer expect very much from them. A barren emptiness comes into our relation with our fellow men, an undermining indifference. On sad occasions we behave sadly, on gay ones gaily, because it is the right thing to do. We start to consider it all not very important. Everything becomes vague. We have only one desire, to sleep—perhaps not exactly physically, but existentially; no longer to fight; to cope with what we have to do as easily as possible, to put on a mask of activity and decency, and sleep behind it. If we woke up, we would have to change everything! Life has become narrowed down in us. Are we to break out again into the world of freedom? Indifference and lassitude come more easily, for in that state we can keep going without effort, rather like a somnambulist. At least our anxiety before that which is greater and makes a total demand on us will go to sleep.

This destructive lukewarmness is like a spiritual anaemia; it is the result of constant giving up. The living quality of life gradually disintegrates. To begin with one does not perhaps notice anything. But suddenly nothing; the trees of our own life do not bear fruit; the fruitful earth has become stone. Even sin has become a habit, a part of our ego that we hate and that we still cannot get rid of. A deathly emptiness starts to engulf us. We are nothing any longer, only tired—of everyone and of ourself. We no longer love life. We are dead men even before we have died.

And so we turn in a circle. The hours pass silent and melancholy. We no longer take sides, we no longer judge the situation, we let others decide about life. We become the silent spectator of our own actions, remote from life, remote from ourselves, in a terrifying absence. A strange habit develops that we find, in its positive form, only with the mystics: we exclude the greater part of our consciousness and manage to do even the most important work using only a minimum of our intellectual and emotional powers. The senses still perceive colour, taste, smell and form, but all these impressions no longer penetrate into our real self. External life now seems to go on as if by itself. We can take part in meetings and conversations, say intelligent things, and even give remarkable lectures. While the mind and lips are doing this work and a man even develops into a well-known and important personality, he remains remote, leads his own life, shut within himself, nowhere working for the benefit of what is greater and more beautiful.

This kind of man can even exercise a great attraction. His fellow men begin to notice him, they think about him, woo him, seek to conquer him, are touched and moved by him, but finally also destroyed. He seeks nobody, but attracts people. This is perhaps the strangest thing about this man who is inwardly hollow. He often radiates an intense power, a power that is without an object, that poisons itself and is impotent. In this kind of man there is a frightful inner coldness, even if he behaves externally in a kind and tender manner. There is such a thing as a powerful and intense cold, a cold passion; ice can burn us also! The men around him suspect mysterious treasures within him. But inside he remains indifferent. There he is empty. Life seems to be "frozen" in him.

This kind of man is a long way away, not only from others, but also from himself. If the heart is not alive, a man stands, as it were, outside himself. This makes for an existential remoteness: people cannot really "penetrate" him, they cannot be intimate with him. He is shut off. But inside him there is nothing that is worth being guarded by this reserve. He is unreachable, "ungivable", he cannot enrich anybody, nor belong to anybody; he cannot receive, he cannot grow rich in that which alone enriches: love that gives itself.

If such a man is present in a group, people feel perhaps a fascinating power; but at the same time there is something in this man that is not alive. He exists, but does not experience life. He thinks, but he does not follow through the thought. He has an effect on men, but he does not experience human relationships. His gifts, his abstract genius can excite others in a way that inflames their whole being, but afterwards he simply throws them away, he dishonours them and destroys what is great in them.

Let us not pursue this "negative phenomenology" any further. There are various things that could be added here, but it can be left to each of us to examine his own conscience. We were simply tracing the descending line that leads down into inner lifelessness, and indicating some elements of the danger to which we are all exposed: namely, the dishonouring of life. Perhaps our most important task in the world before God is to overcome this inner emptiness. We should let life itself mature in us until it gains its full form in us and about us.

Reverence for our neighbour

Another human being is not immediately "given" to us. We must constantly seek him out anew, out of fidelity and in trust. But what justifies this trust? Only trust itself. It hardly can be justified. This is where greatness lies, the great "nevertheless" of reverence, or, put more simply, trust in life. If, despite all disappointment, a man persists with another person, then slowly something grows that gives help, radiates goodness and brings hope. Suddenly there is a new promise. The world experiences through us that it is alive, beautiful and worthy of affirmation. Being becomes happy only if we experience it as happiness, and only in such a way that it notices that we are made happy by it. Selfless reverence is making others happy by experiencing their being as happiness.

We revere the being of others simply by receiving it, without any other motive. This can take place only in a silent, but increasingly intense act of persistently being open to the being of the other. We do not wait for others to confirm our being first, to seek us out, but we are concerned first for them, caring for them and helping them. This quiet receptivity and this active caring create more brightness and light in the world.

There is something in this attitude of a strange defencelessness, from which, however, there flows power; that selflessness that accepts fate, that does not judge or condemn, by its very nature. It simply accepts the life of others without anything of our own claims, or our own self-assertion or feelings being involved. By affirming the whole existence of others, this selflessness becomes a constructive power. It does not reach out beyond the present into the impossible and the utopian, but tries to awaken life, to create a way out of apparently hopeless situations. We try to think for others, to weigh things up, judge situations and smooth a way.

It is moving to see how life flourishes if we trust it; how men change if we put a greater value on them (and treat them accordingly); if we prove to them by our quiet, discreet reverence that they have within themselves things that are good, beautiful and lovable, something that lives in them as a promise, but must be developed. Without hope of greatness life perishes. Pierre Teilhard de Chardin writes well about this:

> Let so-called exact and critical thinkers say that the new generation is less naïve than the last and no longer believes in a future and in the world being made perfect. Have the people who write such things thought of the fact that all movement of the mind would cease on earth if they were right? They seem to believe that life would calmly go on even if it were robbed of light, hope, and the lure of an inexhaustible future. Perhaps it would still produce blooms and fruits for a few years out of sheer habit. But its trunk would already be separated from the roots. Even if mankind had enormous amounts of material energy available, without this love of life it would soon no longer want to work at a task that it knew was hopelessly damned. Wounded in the source of its energy, disgust or rebellion would make mankind disintegrate and fall to dust.

This teaches us that hope, a fundamental optimism, the "taste for happiness", constitutes the true element in which man lives. It is an essential part of the human day—and in a double sense—that it starts as *"Morgen"*. In German this word means both "morning" and "tomorrow". It is both what arrives fresh, driving away the night, and what is to come, that which lies behind today, in the future. It is liberation from oppressive mustiness, a break-through into fresh air and wide expanses that fosters life. *"Incipit vita nova"*—new life begins ("here we go")—is how Dante expressed the basic mood of man as he grows into life. Paul used similar words: "We . . . walk in newness of life" (Rom. 6. 4). Man's being expands in a mood of high courage. This is the secret spur of the soul, the stretching out of the spirit towards those great things that have yet to come. The ancients called it the *"extensio animi ad magna"*. To preserve this openness to the greater in men and even to nourish it is reverence.

But can another man so step out of himself, be so liberated? How do I make another man someone who raises himself up? How do I hold my friends open? How do I teach them that life begins now and that the process of a man becoming human is still going on? By recognizing in them something greater, by proving in my attitude to them that their life is on the way towards an absolute fulfilment.

This, incidentally, is the meaning of the sacraments. A sacrament means that an earthly action contains an absolute value, something that is absolutely worthy of reverence. The water with which we daily wash ourselves; the process of developing and maturing; eating together which is the expression of our being together in an inner way; the reversal in contrition of a life that was going in the wrong direction, and a talk that expresses human goodwill, is friendly and guides us; the striving for the absolute and incomprehensible; the love that involves body and soul, the succour of one's fellow, faithfully lived sexuality; helping the sick or suffering or dying, and generally the honest fulfilling of our daily, given life—all this contains infinite mysteries and thus an absolute value. The sacraments mean that our life is moving towards an absolute, that man contains within himself a self-transcendence, a capacity to surpass himself which he will never exhaust and which is the only thing that makes him a man. We proclaim all the sacraments, in fact we bring them—implicitly, that is in an inclusive and anticipatory way—to those men whom we treat with honour, whom we consider capable of more reality and being than they can show.

What are we to bring to others through our reverence to them is not a simple belief in progress. It is faith in an absolute and unsurpassable future which is already alive in us all. It is only in terms of the ineffable and unsurpassable mystery that human development and progress can be affirmed and undertaken. Only in a world that is planned in relation to an absolute perfection is it possible to have human hopes and joys; nothing more can happen to me. Even if I succeed in nothing, even if my life disintegrates, even if I no longer have any prospects, my inner mystery and my absolute future remain untouchable. By entering into this absolute mystery, the essential part of my life is fulfilled.

The Christian should radiate in the world this basic mood of existential serenity, the experience that life is really released.[3] It has an absolute future before it. Let us, therefore, be men who press on with living. This absolute mystery that we bear within ourselves is, moreover, something that is given to us as an individual grace, it is a personal mystery, an irreplaceable charism. I, in my unique life, bear something within me that is irreplaceable: an absolute task to perform. If I fail in the world, if I do not perfect myself as a man, then it is not just that something is missing in the world, but it is obscured, it loses its colour. I am indispensable for the whole world. To prove the indispensability of the other man, in word and deed, in simply being with him, in our whole attitude, that is reverence. It is not yet friendship and love, but it creates in the world a space for these things; it is an all-embracing sympathy for other beings.

If we practise this attitude of fundamental universal sympathy (and we all know how difficult it is), that is, we cultivate the virtue of reverence, we become a person. In the giving and forgetting of ourself there grows in us a new kind of being. By revering another person we become ourself, truly ourself, we become an essential centre, we experience the existential process that we may describe as self-becoming.

Reverence for our own existence

By approaching other men with a reverence that has trust in them and recognizes their unique, absolute quality, we discover that our own life is worthy of being revered. This is a strange process. The personality becomes firm, and at the same time supple. This is what distinguishes us from the animals. An animal is fixed; led by its instincts, it lives se-

---

[3] There is a play on words here in the German: "ausgelassen" means "exuberant", but by hyphenating it the author gives it the participial force of "let out" and also links it with "Gelassenheit", "serenity".—Trans.

curely, fixed in its environment, despite the often fierce struggle for existence. As against this, man seeks from the beginning his place in the world; in this search he often stumbles
and takes the wrong path. He is unstable, eccentric, existentially unfixed, uncertain. This fixing process, the finding of
one's own life, of one's own person we have already called
self-becoming. It takes place by a man discovering the absolute in other men and experiencing reverence for this. Man
becomes essential in recognizing the essential quality in
other men. His own life begins to grow in depth.

Such a man is, as we have already said, himself serene. He
has discovered a dignity, a holy significance in life that cannot
be threatened by any external dangers. Thus he lives in a
quiet equanimity. His balance is not easily upset in the various
situations of life, in suffering and joy, in danger and terrible
happenings. It is often only the people who are close to him
who notice that behind this serenity there is a great glow of
the spirit. It is not consuming, but creative and preserving.

This serenity that has a gay vitality is exactly the opposite
of laziness; it is strength. At the same time the soul is stirred;
it remains inwardly active, alive and open to influences from
many sides. That is why, despite his imperturbability and
equanimity (which is not to be confused with indifference),
such a man remains inwardly mobile. The mobility of his
intellect is seen in his encountering other people with understanding and in his openness to all stimuli; the mobility of
his heart in its compassion and its breadth. Such a man is
"self-confident" and even—in the right sense—"proud", he is
aware of his profoundest dignity, but a dignity that does not
come from him, is not founded in his own being. That is
why this self-revering attitude is always combined with humility, which is not arrogant and which bows before the absolute and before one's fellow men. He shows this humility
in his quiet readiness to make sacrifices. The reality of the
world does not stop him from growing into the infinite, of
giving himself when it is necessary. In this way the man who
reveres others grows in richness, depth and spiritual intensity.

We notice in him a curious kind of activity; he lives and

works, to use a scriptural word, "from the spirit". This is
seen in a clarity and transparency of his being, in his creative
and enriching simplicity. He is one with his fate. It no longer
causes him anxiety. He is beyond the upheavals, the anxieties
and the dangers of life; he lives, as it were, with his fate, and
this lives in him. Thus we can also understand that he has a
particular capacity for friendship, encounter and love. His
being unfolds towards other peoples, because everywhere in
the world he is able to discover the mystery, a mystery in
which he and all other beings are held.

This shows us another characteristic of his life, a certain
melancholy. This is nothing but the experience of the greatness of life and at the same time the profound inadequacy of
our attempts to realize this greatness. Actually this melancholy is only homesickness. It is the pain of the absolute being
born in finite existence, the unrest of man, who has to live
close to the absolute, which he experiences everywhere. It is a
joy and at the same time a threat. Such men experience the
"gulf", a discontinuity on two sides. Their way into everyday
life is interrupted by the fact that they have the responsibility
of an experience of the absolute and what is absolutely to be
revered. And their way to the absolute is interrupted by the
fact that they have to live a life that is essentially imperfect,
as creatures, and are never able to create this absolute out of
themselves. But this is the truly human attitude: an attitude
that is born of the experience of the frontiers of life.

It is easy to speak of this essential melancholy; it is more
difficult to live with it. Melancholy, the intense experience of
the gravity and significance of life, can devalue many things, it
can empty many forms and values, it can make much appear
unreal and drive a man into emptiness and satiety. On the
other hand, the "heavy-minded" man has the deepest relationship to the fullness of life. He is able to see the bright
colourfulness of the world and hear its full harmonies. He is
a man out of whose being the full blood of life bursts and who
is able to experience the boundlessness of all existence. His
life is "supra-finite", that is, striving towards the infinite. In
the very enrichment of his being he experiences his own unful-

fillability, a deeper emptiness, a barrenness of life, and in this, again, longing.

The restless, unstilled quality of life, however, is the proof of the other, of the absolutely other. And thus we are faced with the paradox that a man can only be himself, he can only find his way back to his own being in living, as it were, beyond himself, in experiencing that his fulfillment lies precisely in his being unfulfilled. Since real satisfaction, total stilling of his longing is impossible, he feels a sadness and then longing, a profound nostalgia at the knowledge that a man cannot fulfil his true being from himself.

In order to revere man, one must revere oneself. But one cannot revere oneself without revering something within oneself that absolutely transcends oneself: namely, God.

Reverence for God

Here we shall omit all intermediate stages and come straight to the essential point. There was a man in whom God himself totally revered humanity: Christ. He has affirmed the boundlessness of our existence once and for all. Almost all the important statements of Christ are introduced in the Gospel with the word "amen", "truly". In John we sometimes even find it twice: "Truly, truly, I say to you" (*cf.* John 1. 51; 5. 19). The great affirmation of human reality was expressed in Christ. By simply listing the individual passages in Scripture, we should just like to indicate here how much God, who became man, revered humanity.

"For the Son of God, Jesus Christ, whom we preached among you . . . was not Yes and No; but in him it is always Yes. For all the promises of God find their Yes in him. That is why we utter the Amen through him" (2 Cor. 1. 19f.). He is "a fury of fire which will consume" (Heb. 10. 27), that is, will take man beyond himself. "It is done! I am the Alpha and the Omega, the beginning and the end. To the thirsty I will give water without price from the fountain of the water of life" (Rev. 21. 6). "Whoever drinks of the water that I shall give him will never thirst; the water that I shall give him will become in him a spring of water welling up to eternal life" (John 4. 14). The fullness is there: "Forgetting what lies behind and straining forward to what lies ahead, I press on toward the goal for the prize of the upward call of God in Christ Jesus" (Phil. 3. 13–14). "Grace and truth come through Jesus Christ" (John 1. 17). In him "the goodness and loving kindness of God our Saviour appeared" (Titus 3. 4). He assures us: "Lo, I am with you always, to the close of the age" (Matt. 28. 20). The profoundest longing of man has become reality: "Behold, I send the promise of my Father upon you" (Luke 24. 49). Since this the world is wholly open: "And before him no creature is hidden, but all are open and laid bare to the eyes of him with whom we have to do" (Heb. 4. 13). Absolute love embraces, through Christ, the whole universe: he has united "all things in him, things in heaven and things on earth" (Eph. 1. 10). "It is fitting for us to fulfil all righteousness", he said to John the Baptist, at the beginning of his ministry (Matt. 3. 15). And he really saw it through to the end: "He said, 'It is finished'; and he bowed his head" (John 19. 30). This bowing of his head (into death) was the act of Christ's life. In Christ God said Yes to our whole human nature, in all its pettiness, its nothingness, but at the same time with all its hope and openness to the absolute.

From now on, when a man thinks of the future and, still more, when he reveres life, when he helps life to grow, when he nourishes in himself hope of something still greater, if he has love for life, then he is on his knees, even if he is sitting in a train or standing in a tram. We can never come to the end of thinking about the absolute, about God, about his ways and his decrees.

And yet the man who reveres others has already reached the goal. Whenever he sees the absolute in another and lovingly acknowledges it, this absolute streams back to him and man is borne into the incarnate God. This life is a life in God, and yet precisely because of that a life in the world. He is, to the depths of his being, turned towards God. Precisely through this such a man can pour power and life into the world. They can also be quite simple, even childlike; these men who are truly possessed by Christ are of a strangely enlivening, healing and sanctifying spirit. They are not miracles, but something miraculous appears in them. They live in a state for which early theology had a strange word: *"fruitio Dei"*, "the enjoyment of God". They live in him, perhaps without knowing it, without even thinking about it. In their reverence for God these men have found themselves and their brother.

4. JOY

When I was considering this section on the mystery of Christian joy, I was struck by how quickly man's supply of words runs out when he wants to speak about joy. Language fails him. It sounds hollow and artificial. Only in music can we support a more extended expression of great joy. But even here it may only come as the quick crowning and conclusion of an arduous struggle. On the other hand, how eloquent man is when he describes suffering, pain and misfortune. If one took away these themes from literature, then there would hardly be anything left. It is as if man felt more at home in the abysses of suffering than in the regions of joy. There is a profound truth in this observation: suffering and pain spring directly from our life. The higher and more delicate the development of a creature, the more sensitive he becomes to suffering. Joy, on the other hand, has to be learnt, it has to be practised as a virtue.

True, real joy always comes to us only as a present. It originates in God. Human joy is a share through grace in the joy of God, in God's nature, which is nothing but the sphere of supreme joy. The sources of true joy, therefore, are found where the creature waits for God. Joy is not a part of our existence; nevertheless our existence is completed only in it. That is why the essential part of our existence is grace. Or, as Pascal says: "Man infinitely transcends man." That is why joy cannot be regarded as something ready-made, like something provided externally in the world, in the exterior layers of our being. It is not part of the area of pleasure and distraction. We shall take up this idea again. Here, as with our previous themes, we shall describe the negative condition of joylessness, a situation that is perhaps the commonest experience of our life. What are its ingredients?

First, probably, a tired lack of involvement. There were once in our life times of enthusiasm, of glowing and vital life, of passionate involvement. Now everything is grey and an effort. The fire of desire and longing has somehow gone out. It is laziness, the incapacity of living with a light inside us, the fact that things are easy, all too easy, that makes us so tired. It is not the difficult things that weaken us, but what is all too easy. We no longer seek great things. We rest satisfied with what has been allotted us by a blind fate. "Don't think too much! Don't expect too much! Everyone does things like this! They have always done so!"

We have an irradicable distrust of joy, of novelty. That is why sometimes hard words have to be spoken, why Christ had to speak them, who was wholly love, mildness and mercy, words to shake up us men who are asleep, blunted and indifferent. He had to break through the hard crust of our mediocrity, he had to use the frightful hammer of his word. He had to break open the prison of our uncaring attitude to life in which we suffocate, die of thirst and grow blind. He never spoke a "pious", soporific language. He never reproached those who were possessed. He liberated them. Perhaps the contemporary possession is nothing but a tired lack of involvement, the existential disappointment and lack of strength of our age. Perhaps the possessed of today are tortured by the power of joylessness.

We have to be very careful: lack of involvement is a gentle slope down which one can slide almost imperceptibly, and no life, no profession, no temperament, not even sanctity is free of its danger. Tiredness and sadness: where do they come from? First from quite small causes: too much work, no security, debts, separation, loneliness, sickness, set-backs, incompatibility of faith with hard reality, unfulfillable morality, a Church that is disappointed. . . . The list could be continued endlessly. Life has so many limitations, disappointments and impossibilities. We are only tired and absent. Above all absent from ourselves. The worst thing is that when one is sunk so deep in absence one can no longer be conscious of one's condition. Happy is he who recognizes his unhappiness, suffers from it, he who can really be unhappy and not just simply limp.

This tired lack of involvement creates in our being a profound lack of confirmation, a dangerous dissatisfaction. We are dissatisfied with everything. We feel as if we had no being, as if we were no one. This is why we seek with nervous haste for self-confirmation, stimuli, experiences, riches. We plunge into external things in order to forget ourselves, precisely because we cannot really forget ourselves. We live in a state of mind in which everything appears in a sombre light. There is no healthy climate of thought and feeling.

This gives rise to existential flatness. Life somehow becomes all on one level. It is easy to live an uninvolved, unconfirmed and unhappy life; it takes no effort. To be happy we have to exert ourselves. What can still really take place in a joyless life can equally well happen to other people. In joylessness human life becomes universally livable. Nothing unique ever happens.

This explains the fact that a joyless life is a mediocre one. This kind of man lives in a world that may perhaps function well, but it is flat. Joy and promise are enviously put aside. Any question of fighting for things with one's heart is regarded as an illusion, and those things are worked for that are tangible, that can be attained and possessed. The world is reduced to a wretched state: everything is uniformly grey, ordinary, graspable and has its price; what is new is pushed aside with a tired movement of the hand and is declared unimportant and unserious.

Joyless life becomes heavy and opaque. Life becomes commonplace. It is no longer felt that a being can be more than an appearance. But only the mysterious is supportable in the long run; we can really love only that which has mystery about it. Only a thing that one can control can be without mystery, not a person to whom one looks up. Wherever man experiences true joy, he also directly experiences mystery. In a world without mystery and without joy, however, life lacks relationships. Words lose their meaning. They no longer bring things close, but, rather, push them away. We have talking without an object, a flood of meaningless words.

This kind of life cannot be borne. That is why the joyless man plunges into existential restlessness. Such a man, who has emptied and devalued his world, no longer finds any place for wonder, for amazed lingering and remaining. He no longer rests anywhere in his life. However many things he chases after, he finds everywhere the same quality of negligence, lack of confirmation, mediocrity and meaninglessness. This is the reason for the "bad" dissatisfaction that we have mentioned (there is also a good one), the reason for the unrest, the excitement, curiosity, inconstancy and distraction. The joyless man would like to be everywhere and, in reality, is nowhere.

In the long run, this kind of life leads to exhaustion. There is nothing more that allows for daring, for self-sacrifice and responsibility. Life becomes dull-hearted and lazy, tired and blunted, depressed and petty. The man who unloads work becomes tired; but he who freely accepts the "burden of joy" becomes light and young.

Joy in one's brother

True joy is not a fanatical enthusiasm that is remote from the world, nor is it an inner emigration. Quite the contrary. In detaching ourselves from ourselves and going to our brother, we experience joy. Only giving ourselves to others creates the courage to embrace reality, creates that closeness of heart to everything, that gentle light over everything that we describe by the word "joy". The way of joy leads via selflessness. We have to destroy in ourselves something of our involvement with ourselves, our laziness and our negative feeling states. And to the extent that we try to move out of our enslavement to pettiness, we will find that something moves in us that is like a power, a hidden vitality. Finally we discover it in ourselves, like the last glimmer of a flame, long hidden embers that again begin to burn as soon as they receive a little air. It is the same when we open ourselves towards our brother. The simple service of our brother in everyday life is the necessary precondition of joy. On the day of the ascension of the Lord, after Christ had disappeared from their gaze, the disciples went away with great joy. We learn this from the gospel of St Luke. A strange joy! The face of the Lord withdrew from their eyes and their senses, and with him the glory that they had directly experienced. The hearts of the disciples had already before been moved with joy, when the mysterious light of glory shone on them from the face of Christ on the first day of Easter week. On that occasion the event of Easter had brought about a new closeness of the Lord, seen and experienced only—as I imagine—by the inner senses. In the face of Jesus there was the radiance of God, the radiance of the kingdom of God, the radiance of the great reconciliation and mercifulness. This was the light that "shone brighter than the sun and more purely than snow". And the hearts of the disciples were changed. The ineffable touches them and their hearts burnt within them.

But on the day of the ascension an even more significant transformation took place. Precisely through the departure of Christ the joy of the disciples reached full measure, it moved into a new stage of perfection and maturity. And thus they went back with great joy into their little world. Wholly withdrawn from the senses, the Lord had now moved out of the narrowness of human ideas and imaginings, he had moved fully into that which no eye had seen, no ear heard, and what had not penetrated into the heart of any man. Against all the tendencies of human beings the disciples had suddenly realized that from now on they had to seek joy in the invisible that is behind all that is visible, that is, that they could find joy everywhere, because Christ is present everywhere. From now on man is no longer to stare up at the sky amazedly, but to take up his earthly tasks in order to find joy. This made his brother the source of joy. Thus the disciples began to experience in life that the invisible and the ineffable is to be found in the visible.

The same thing happens from time to time among us men also. When we are touched by the power of friendship or love, then our senses begin to perceive the invisible. At the ascension of Christ the disciples had simply a universal human experience (though in a supreme form): the Lord had parted from them (Christ moved into an all-cosmic presence), and in this they realized that everywhere in the world there lives something that cannot be plumbed, something mysterious, something that illuminates and makes joyful. But when absolute joy—Christ—departed from them, it came absolutely near to them. From now on they need do nothing else but detach themselves from themselves, go to their brother; in this way they find joy and complete happiness. Christ's ascension was undoubtedly an inner event; an event that did not concern Christ himself, but is intended to affect our hearts. His resurrection was already an ascension. Christ went, as a man, to the place, where, as the second divine person, he always was: into the glory of God. Thus he did not need to "go to heaven". But it was necessary for us to experience—in an extreme moment of realization—that he departed from us, that is, that, if we want to find joy and fulfilment, we also must go away from ourselves. Christ's ascension reveals the basic structure of real joy: the departure from one's self.

The ascension led the disciples into the world: that means, out of themselves. They went to Jerusalem, they chose Matthias, they preached at Pentecost, they experienced the difficult conflict with their own people, they underwent the inner tensions of the Church community in its slow and quiet growth; they went out into all the world and faced all the difficulties. Thus they became ever more deeply involved in the problem, the suffering, the conflict of the world, they experienced daily more and more its tribulations and its dark ways. Nothing was spared them, and they did not spare themselves. But the invisible joy remained. Above the sufferings, above poverty, above the meanness and guilt they saw with the eyes that see the invisible, the spirit of reconciliation and of eternal grace. The spirit of joy was in the world. The joy of God went its way with the apostles over the earth. "I am filled with comfort. With all our affliction, I am overjoyed" (2 Cor. 7. 4). Thus we have found the basic law of human joy: *Involving ourselves in the suffering of our brother*, taking his burden upon us, helping to carry his cross. This is the way to happiness: silent service and help, creating joy in the world.

Joy in our own being

We experience joy in the measure that we give it. This is the result of our thinking so far. Hence joy is the fruit of a conscious endeavour, a constant detachment from one's self. It is difficult to be joyful in our world. Let us now consider the essential passages from the revelation of the new covenant, that is, the good news, which is for us the basis of joy.

On the one hand we have: "Another said, 'I will follow you, Lord; but let me first say farewell to those at my home.' Jesus said to him, 'No one who puts his hand to the plough and looks back is fit for the kingdom of God'" (Luke 9. 61–62). "Do not be anxious about tomorrow, for tomorrow will be anxious for itself. Let today's own trouble be sufficient for today" (Matt. 6. 34). "If any man would come after me, let him deny himself and take up his cross and follow me" (Mark 8. 34). "Whoever would save his life will lose it; and whoever loses his life for my sake . . . will save it" (Mark 8. 35).

On the other hand we have the fact that this detachment from one's self brings an inner serenity into Christian living, it stimulates joy and repentance. Here we should consider the extraordinary events of which the gospels constantly tell us: the joy of Zacchaeus, the chief tax collector, who climbed down from the tree and joyfully took Christ to his home (Luke 19. 1–10); but also we learn of the murmuring of the so-called righteous men against Christ because he ate with sinners (Mark 2. 15–17); and again we have the contrite sinner with her alabaster flask (Luke 7. 36–50); we have the parables of the lost sheep and the lost coin (Luke 15. 4–7; 8–10); the story of the prodigal son who returned home (Luke 15. 11–32); and, above all, the extraordinary fact that the lord of the vineyard paid the same wages to those whom he had hired at the eleventh hour as to those who had borne the burden and the heat of the whole day (Matt. 20. 1–16).

Thus, on the one hand, total sacrifice is asked of us, and, on the other, God accepts the smallest sign of self-sacrifice as a total giving. A commandment and a liberation at the same time. Although it seems absurd at first sight, it is true that in life the way of joy passes through renunciation. But this means that all renunciation serves fulfilment; all mortification takes place in order to make alive. To praise suffering and denial as ultimates would indeed be foolish. There is already enough suffering in the world. But detachment from ourselves in the cause of brotherly service makes what is apparently impossible possible. Even in the almost intolerable suffering man can still be happy, provided that he is not seeking his own happiness. The saints speak of their overwhelming joy, they even shout and sing in the middle of the most terrible external tribulations. Francis of Assisi had to pick up two pieces of wood and play on them as if they were a fiddle and bow, he had to dance and sing. And Francis Xavier, for sheer joy, threw an apple in the air and caught it again, like a child at play, when, bereft of everything and beset by failure, he was walking through the fields of Japan covered with the ice of winter. We experience joy only in opening ourselves, in embracing, in giving ourselves. If all we do is hang on to ourselves, then everything distresses us that in any way attacks this self: sickness, suffering, poverty, dishonour and failure. But if we have given ourselves to the service of our brother, if we have handed over our self to our neighbour, everything that we undergo ourselves becomes totally unimportant.

Joy given by God

Christian joy that penetrates everything became possible, as we have already seen, by the fact that Christ through his ascension became all in all to us. We can wholly move away from ourselves and face all situations of life; everywhere we encounter him, everywhere we find him who has promised us exceeding joy. In order, therefore, to describe Christian joy, this serenity of the believer's life, we must consider further what took place in the ascension of Christ.

In the account of the ascension that Luke has given us in the Acts of the Apostles and at the end of his gospel, we find two main elements that determine our whole Christian situation in the world: the disciples look after Christ and want to move, as it were, with him out of the world. But at the same time the angel of the Lord appears to them and tells them to direct their gaze towards the earth and pursue their earthly task. Clement of Alexandria expressed this basic tension of Christian life at the beginning of the third century in the following way in his *Stromata*: the perfect Christian is both "of the world and above the world". This is an exact description of the reality that was opened up to us through the ascension of Christ.

Above the world: The Christian must be convinced that his life is unimportant, that there follows on it an eternal state of happiness and joy. He must not take everything too seriously, only what might prevent him from attaining eternal life. For him nothing is big enough. He cannot be impressed. On the face of a Christian there should always be a gentle smile which says: Don't be so pompous, don't take yourselves so seriously; everything passes; basically, nothing can happen to us; the best thing would be to go straight to Christ; don't let anyone deceive you, the others have to take themselves seriously, for often it is all they have; in reality it is all quite unimportant and has no significance; we live out of a God that is beyond the whole world and we live into him; in our hope, that is, with the longing of our Christian heart, we are already with him; and thus our life cannot be upset by anything. Our fulfilment lies beyond anything that this world offers. Here we have no lasting abode. Christ has taken our life with him. From this superiority of the Christian to the world, from his being above the world, it is clear that the same Christian must enter into the world, so much so that he can almost forget about heaven in the process.

Of the world: Only if this is his attitude can he take the world seriously. It is not honour, success, self-righteousness and self-enrichment that advance the world, but that which is done out of pure human goodness. But a man is capable of this only if these things have become unimportant for him. Because God is greater than everything, he can be found everywhere, even in the most insignificant things. He can meet us on every path. That is why, fundamentally, everything in the world is important. So important that Ignatius of Loyola was able to say: "If God were to say to me: 'If you want to die now, I would give you paradise at once, but if you want to go on living on earth, then you live at your own risk', then I would answer: 'I would rather remain in this life with the risk, only so that I could do God an even greater service.'" This attitude gives rise to a constant readiness to hear the call of God in every situation in the world, an all-embracing capacity to serve our neighbour, an openness of our hearts towards everything that exists and lives.

On this basis a "spirituality of the ascension" could be evolved, as the ultimate attitude of the Christian towards reality. This attitude is twofold.

First: The Christian is to be boundless in everything that is great. God is always greater. We are satisfied by nothing that is not God. Our life—both here on earth and in eternity —is a never-ending march forward into the unbounded. Every fulfilment is only the fulfilment of a further search. That is why the Christian must always be ready for a new task. He must have the courage to be discontented. He has the duty of finding a lasting resting-place nowhere in this ceaseless journey towards his rest in God. Within him there must be a holy dissatisfaction. He is to test all the possibilities, leave no paths untried, constantly make new plans. Whatever is achieved is finished for him, simply because it is achieved. Only what has not yet been achieved is worthy of being attacked. Thus man remains open to God and to his constantly new call, he does not tie himself to means that have been chosen once and for all. The greatest, most beautiful and most sacred things are not great, beautiful or sacred enough for him. To put it paradoxically, he does not let himself be limited by anything great. His longing is always still greater than the greatest realization.

Secondly, however: He should seek his great God everywhere, that is, even in the smallest things. Quietly, calmly and modestly he should fulfil the task that God has allotted him, because in this very smallness he finds the God that is always greater. He should use everything, even the most inadequate means, if he can render a service with it. He is to hide the greatness of his eternal longing within the tiny framework of earthly fulfilment. His longing is always open at the top, turned towards what is always greater. The full measure of his being is boundlessness. And yet this longing must always remain enclosed within the smallness of what can be reached on earth.

The man who is able to combine both things in his life, the measurelessness of the great and the narrowness of the small is living the ascension of Christ in his own human reality. "Not to be restricted by the greatest and yet to remain enclosed in the smallest"—this is how we can best describe the "ascension attitude" of the Christian. Rest in restlessness, peace in peacelessness, the acceptance of one's own limitations in constant longing for the boundless, being satisfied with the most insignificant things and always striving for what is more perfect: this is the attitude that has become, in the ascension of Christ, the basic law of holiness. The tension between heaven and earth is summed up in such a man. In him heaven passes into the earthly, and the earthly achieves in him an eternal existence. Such a man rejoices with his whole being. Man exists as joy. From God.

From the practice of these two qualities of human authenticity, reverence and joy, grows *service*, joyful, helpful assistance, the lively, watchful and healing creation of a new lightness in the world, the readiness to stay quietly with a suffering creature. The life of Jesus was one of constant fidelity to help and service. It was expressed in the fact that he persisted all his life in a narrow and inimical environment, in a cruel corner of our earth, dispensing comfort, rest, and inner peace, although the wide pagan world would probably have welcomed him far more rapidly.

One final thought which sums up all we have said so far and leads us to our next section: a man of deep experience

who spent many years in a Siberian concentration camp once
wrote something that fully expressed existential authenticity:
"I sought my God, and he withdrew from me; I sought my
soul and I did not find it; I sought my brother, and I found all
three."

5. FRIENDSHIP

We cannot speak about friendship and love, these "ultimate things" of life, according to a preconceived scheme. In the world of today that is so often without friendship and love we have to learn them anew from men who have deeply experienced their reality. Thus we have chosen two texts which express, for us, the true greatness of friendship and love. The first is to be found in the tenth chapter of St Augustine's *Confessions*:

> When the day was approaching on which she was to depart this life . . . it came about, as I believe, by your secret arrangement, that she and I stood alone leaning in a window, which looked inwards to the garden within the house where we were staying, at Ostia on the Tiber, for there we were away from everybody, resting for the sea-voyage from the weariness of our long journey by land. There we talked together, she and I alone, in deep joy . . . we were discussing . . . what the eternal life of the saints could be like. And higher still we soared, thinking in our minds and speaking and marvelling at your works: and so we came to our own souls, and went beyond them to come at last to the region of riches unending. . . . And while we were thus talking of His Wisdom and panting for it, with all the effort of our heart, did for one instant attain to touch it; then sighing, . . . we returned to the sound of our own tongue, in which a word has both beginning and ending.

This is the text. It is an extraordinary event which took place between mother and son, but it can also be regarded as a description of growth in awareness between two people, that is, of what takes place in every friendship.

On first reading the text we note that in friendship there

is a kind of knowing, a mutual knowing. Two persons become aware of each other; their whole being has the same "vibration". In friendship one's life is taken hold of by another person. But at the same time this includes the fact that in the same act our life is also taken hold of by the absolute. In order to understand we must simply start to cultivate friendship, to take the risk of friendship, in order to experience in it, precisely in the being together of two finite beings, the attraction of the absolute. This knowledge of the other being is by no means theoretical, but takes place as a direct awareness, as an existential resting of a man in a strange being. For this our eyes must become simple, even childlike. This proceeds only from an inner calm. And in this quiet being together, in this "standing together" at the window there is at the same time an inner knowledge of God. When two men are with each other in friendship they sense the presence of the absolute, of God.

This text of Augustine is among the small number of those documents of the inner life that contain an indestructible living power and are able to offer criteria for living. It reproduces an experience of the highest intensity. It is a testimony of personal history in the strictest sense of the word, and at the same time, or precisely for that reason, familiar to us all from our own experiences. There are such moments in the life of every one of us. Sometimes we even remember the exact date of these experiences, and when we think back we can still recapture the taste of the inner transformation—just as Augustine, who knows exactly, years later, at what window they stood when they knew God together. Suddenly and unexpectedly there springs up an intense spiritual bond between two persons, and at the same time the soul of each experiences the absolute.

Let us consider seven basic points from the passage in order to show what can take place in genuinely lived human friendship.

When the day was approaching on which she was to depart this life. First, historically: Monica's life was marked by a strong religious motherliness, which enfolded the growing

Christian life of Augustine and carried it through to conscious existence. In the ninth book of the *Confessions* Augustine tells the profound effect that the death of his mother had on him. He himself also died in some way with his mother: "My soul was wounded, and my life, as it were, torn in pieces, which till then had been composed of hers and mine."

Augustine's experience shows clearly that friendship is more than simply being together. A friend is a part of my own being. If he is no longer there, then I have somehow died with him. But does not the threat of separation hang over every friendship? What a daring thing it is, then, to enter upon a friendship, to make another person an essential part of our own life! With every separation, every departure—it does not always have to be death—something of ourself dies also. This gives a certain gravity to every genuine friendship: if you no longer exist, if you go away, I am somehow annihilated. And at the point of this inner involvement every friendship touches on a limit; it is laid hold of by the absolute.

Here we have touched on something ultimate in friendship: as long as there is friendship, there is also the experience of the absolute, of God. In friendship there takes place unconsciously a move towards the whole of being. This gives it the character of transcendency. When two beings become aware of each other, they transcend each other. We shall consider this later in more detail, but let us note here the point that the presence of the absolute in the world is existentially sustained through friendship. In friendship there takes place an illumination of our whole life. Through friendship the things of the world carry an extra amount of light, they project, as it were, out of the light of God into reality. Friendship can be the unconscious realization of the presence of the absolute in the world. This is the real, but also the most hidden process of growth in human awareness. Let us describe this event in more detail by giving a further interpretation of the vision of Ostia.

She and I stood alone leaning in a window. They were dwelling in the safety of the house and looking out into the unsafe world. As they leaned at the window, happy and at one with one another, they became aware of the external world. As they looked together the world acquired a quality of communalness, of friendship. There can be a genuine view of things only in a lived and experienced intersubjectivity, in friendship. The moving thing about the story is the attempt of two people, one helping the other, to reach forward to the uttermost boundary of life. Neither of them could make the journey alone. But in fact neither leads, neither the mother nor the son, but both lead and both follow. In friendship there is no precedence. This kind of conversation begins perhaps with unimportant words and then suddenly, as if unintentionally, takes an unexpected direction and arrives at the point at which bliss is experienced. Augustine calls the conversation "most loving". The encounter of friends with the absolute takes place in an atmosphere of gentleness, charm, acceptance and peace. The most delicate thing has the greatest power. The unconditional gives itself to us as grace, as "charis", which also means loveliness and becomes visible for us on the face of our friend.

Dante knew how to express this mysterious quality with poetic and intellectual power. In the twenty-eighth canto of the *Paradiso* he describes in a few words a shattering event. Beatrice stands, turned towards Dante with a loving smile on her face and draws with her beauty the whole of Dante's power of sight. But when the poet looks at Beatrice, he shudders, for he sees how God himself is reflected in her eyes, surrounded by a fiery circle of angels—the purest symbol of the fullness of being that can be experienced in the friendship of two fragile earthly beings.

Away from everybody. Here Augustine shows us a new feature of lived friendship. It contains two elements:

Being with another person. Friendship is essentially being with someone. The strange thing about it is that it is almost impossible to say why one has this friend in particular as a friend. If we take all our feelings for another person, all our respect, sympathy, admiration or reverence, the sum of these still does not produce friendship. In friendship man discovers the uniqueness of the other person. He says: It is good that you exist. He separates this person from the crowd of other human relationships.

But why is it a good thing for the friend that the other person exists? It does not make him any richer, he does not gain any advantages through it, he will not advance more quickly in his career. No, it is not in this way that it is good that the friend exists. Do we call him a friend because we can be happy with him, because he wants something from us, because we feel free with him? This also. But this is not the essential thing about friendship. In friendship we do not get something concrete, a thing. Man gets himself back. Before he had this friend he was not, as it were, himself. He was only those roles that he played, that he had to play in the world. The other person, the friend, has the same experience with him. Both exist because they exist with each other, because they are able to say "we". This means something inestimable: the one receives himself from the other in a mutual present. Their being is now a being together. They make up a unity of being. The being of one becomes the material for the other's being, and *vice versa*. From this comes the almost strange demand of friendship to keep one's own being pure, to destroy our own fallenness, selfishness, will to power, laziness of heart and evil, so that all the confusion of one's own being does not pass over to the other person, so that it does not infect or poison him. Thus in friendship there is—often only unconsciously—a constant purification.

Seclusion. It is not by chance that Augustine notes that these two loving human beings had withdrawn from the crowd. The two people like being together and do not want to be disturbed by others. Behind this attitude of withdrawal there is something more profound. External seclusion is only a sign of a qualitative event of the removal of both from other people and, in this, of reserve. The fullness of authentic being reveals itself only to a man who shows towards being a polite reserve, and one learns this only in friendship. Newman called this attitude "the knowledge of the gentleman". It is the aristocratic attitude of a man who does no harm to any being. In it expediency, pretence and hardness of heart are overcome.

Only in this kind of pure, unselfish and relaxed attitude, in the reserve that we learn only in friendship, do we understand things properly. We acquire a calm, relaxed and serene way of looking at the world. What does its ugliness matter to me, or my own sadness and tiredness, my inner littleness? I have a friend who understands me, whose friendship means much more to me than all the offences and disagreeable things that I have to experience daily. In this way our life becomes detached, and we acquire a serene attitude towards things. This inner seclusion is not a rejection. Quite the contrary. Only through friendship do we become truly aware of the inner beauty of things. Inner relaxation lets the sacredness of things shine out from within, it creates the full form of reality. Now we can understand why Augustine says in his narrative: *We were discussing what the eternal life of the saints could be like.*

The shared life of Augustine and Monica is directed towards something eternal. This is characteristic of every friendship. In friendship there is an unconditional affirmation of being. Its essence consists in saying: You shall be! You shall unfold all the potentialities of your being; you shall even become still more beautiful, more radiant, more powerful and more alive than you are; you are the world for me; I experience the world truly only in the light of our friendship; a world without you would be a world without beauty for me. This is the real word of love. In *La mort de demain* Gabriel Marcel makes a character say: "Loving means saying: You will not die." The same thing can be said of friendship. In every profound human relationship, whether it be love or friendship, immortality is also affirmed, posited and included. It cannot be that this being should perish. In human friendship we have direct evidence of immortality and thus a direct sense of a fulfilment in eternity.

We see—not from ourselves, but from the other person— that life must exist eternally, that there must be a condition of ultimate radiance. For Augustine and Monica this state of *"vita beata"* was no utopian sphere of being, but quite exactly and concretely the life of the saints: "Heaven".

Heaven is the inner dynamic of every friendship. In every friendship heaven is already perceived—perhaps in a broken reflection, but nevertheless in a real way. To renounce the total perfecting of friendship would mean not only renouncing the essential thing of friendship, but killing this friendship in the bud. What is the point of totally affirming each other if this affirmation can never develop to a stage of totality? Without the affirmation of heaven as well—whether a man expressly knows about it or not—there can be no live friendship. But this means basically that without heaven it is impossible to live on the earth. In friendship we prove to the world and to ourselves that there must be such a thing as fulfilment in eternity. Thus friendship could be described as a foreknowledge of heaven. Heaven is part of the essential nature of every experience of friendship, even if the friends are often not able to give an account of it, or at least not explicitly.

Here we could perhaps refer again to the friendship of the Emmaus disciples. They remained together. They had given up everything and fled; but they had not given up each other. Where we hold firm to a human friendship right to the end, even to the point of all our dreams and hopes being shattered, the God that we considered so far off is very near to us. Those disciples had not ceased to speak to each other and to be with each other. And thus they gave Christ the chance of joining in their conversation. In this strange event Christ is telling us: Hold fast to your friendship, to your destiny with another human being; if you can still say the word "Thou" you are not lost. It is always possible that when you speak this word it will suddenly be me with whom you are speaking.

The Emmaus disciples are a symbol of our situation in the world today. The greatest chance for man today is friendship honestly lived. Even if friendship is not a sacrament in the strict sense, we can nevertheless be sure that it is a concrete sign of the presence of the absolute in the world, that is, that it realizes everything that we may expect of a sacrament. In our redeemed world the sacramental, the Christ-bearing, is not restricted to the seven sacraments. These are only, as it were, "points of concentration" of the presence of the risen Christ. There are other places of encounter with the Lord, which can be just as effective, even more so than the actual sacraments.

Heaven, the essentiality of being, where everything achieves its full authenticity, is already close to us in friendship. Friends experience it everywhere, perhaps only unconsciously. Thus friendship arouses longing.

We were . . . panting for it. The longing of friendship that springs from the experience of the absolute is at the same time the experience of a basic threat. In the radiance of friendship we sense that we do not yet live in a whole world, that we are not yet in our true place, that the doors of our being are still strangely shut. Aroused by friendship to the light of being, we experience the painful fact that we always sense more than we understand, and that we always feel more than we actually possess. What we have achieved, what we have already realized, has become inwardly empty for us, simply because we have achieved it. This existential disappointment is part of the nature of friendship.

The disappointment of friendship that consists primarily in the fact that we are never sufficiently friends to our friends, that we constantly fail in the honesty and truth of friendship, reaches very deeply into our life. It is a disappointment that has its origin in our experience of the totality of the world. It occurs when a man senses in intimate conversation with a friend the radiance of being, when he has thought that he now holds in his hands the ultimate truth that makes him happy. The next day he finds that it has all flown away, dissolved, and is no longer there. He is like the man who stretches out his hand in a dream towards a visible object and touches nothing; or the man in the story who looks into a mirror and does not see a face in it. In Rilke's *Sonnets to Orpheus* he says: "We were dismissed at the very point where we expected to be greeted."

Maurice Blondel, in his *Action*, one of the most important outlines of modern philosophy, considered the dynamic components of his dissatisfaction which is part of every experience, including friendship: it is the absolute quality of our longing, precisely that which rouses our longing, which is the reason for our existential disappointment; with our boundless longing only God can satisfy us, and only a God of supernatural fulfilment. No human friendship is enough for us. The nature of the friend is only to arouse an absolute longing, that is, to be a predecessor; in his finite and imperfect being a transcendental beyond opens up to us. Our friendship is always just a sign and a symbol, a mountain with many invisible peaks, doors that open as in a dream, in order to show a further strip of carpet and another door. Perhaps we are only "preliminary images"[4] to one another, and the sadness that sometimes is felt between friends comes from a profound disappointment during our search for the absolute.

To be seized by the absolute that shines through the friend, to be carried up by it into the boundless and to realize at the same time that the other person whose being we so totally affirm is still not fulfilment: this is the great sadness, but also the happiness of friendship. To sense the infinite in the finite, this is the nature of friendship.

And . . . with all the effort of our heart, we did for one instant attain to touch it. Augustine now describes the breakthrough to the absolute that takes place in friendship with an image of rising. Platonism, by which the whole of Augustine's thinking was deeply influenced, made the experience of height practically into a system of thought. There is a height that can be reached only by the greatest exertion of soul, with a soaring flight of the spirit, with boldness of feeling, with Platonic "eros". In every genuine experience the human heart rises towards this "metaphysical place" that lies beyond everything. True being, the absolute, can be touched

---

[4] A play on words: "Vor-bilder" also suggests the idea of "models". —Trans.

only by what the Platonic thinkers and mystics have described as the "point of the spirit", the "blade of the mind", the "sharp edge of existence".

This is a profound human experience: to come up into the light, to climb above the mists of our life. But actually Augustine is speaking here of the ultimate touching of our life by the wholly other, by the sacredness of the absolute; he speaks of the spirit glowing in the fire of the encounter with God. He says that this event is "thought" and takes place "in a full beat of the heart".

Our friend is the place of the encounter with the absolute; but this encounter cannot become a lasting state. That is why friendship does not exist as something simply pre-given. It must constantly be built up and won again in fidelity. It is only for a moment that we ever sense truth, that which enlivens our being. But in persisting in friendship for another human being, these moments of the experience of the absolute become more frequent. Our heart, that is, our glowing existence, beats in friendship "up towards" the absolute. There is no other description of this event: we experience God only in our own heart, that is, all we know about him is that our heart, stimulated by our friend, beats "up towards" something that is wholly other. But this is enough for us. We now know that God must be true fullness of meaning, the one and the infinite: we experience him precisely in this hopeless endeavour of friendship that is unfulfillable on this earth. We know that he exists, when in friendship, in its earthly imperfectibility, in our naked, distracted and unfulfilled condition, we have the experience that our unsatisfied heart beats towards a something that is wholly other. We do not know much more about God. This is essentially the structure of our experience of him: the sense of the absolute in the apparently blind mirror of our life, a life that nevertheless becomes a real mirror through friendship.

We returned to the sound of our own tongue. If, after these spiritual moments of "soaring", we again come into contact with ordinary everyday life, our soul experiences a great disappointment, the feeling of intolerable emptiness. The world of the essential seems strange, weak and immature in a world of the everyday and the ordinary. We cannot explain to anyone what a friend has given us. If we begin to formulate in words the true nature of our experience of friendship, our words sound hollow and unreal. We are almost ashamed of exposing it to other men. This feeling of unreality can become so powerful that we can wonder whether we have not deceived ourselves. This makes us uncertain. The true lover is always uncertain. This is his greatness. Sometimes, in one of those blessed moments that restore his courage and confidence, he succeeds in achieving inner certainty. After the first experience of friendship and, in friendship, of the absolute, we should consider calmly and prayerfully what increase of being we have received from the friendship, what took place in it, why we as men—precisely in this encounter—were carried out beyond our limited humanity into the boundless. It can lead to despair to have human friendships; and yet there is no other way to the absolute. This is the way that our human life is structured. It is necessary to hold both things together: friendship and total openness to God. At bottom these two things are but one.

Friendship bursts the bounds of one's own self, and this is painful. In love the other becomes my own self. In this way his suffering also becomes a part of my own being. Every blow that hits him hits me also. As well as my own wretchedness I now have to bear his shortcomings, his failures, his weariness and his cares. We have to persevere faithfully in this unity of being. We also have to accept the consequences of friendship. Friendship can also become a difficult bond that wears us out. Sometimes we have to watch the disintegration of the other person and still keep giving ourselves to him, in a creative way. To do this, even when no longer supported by our own inner *élan*, even when utterly weary and fed up, even when our own life is becoming more and more colourless, even when our heart fails us—all this is genuine, honestly lived friendship. There is no happy friendship, just as there is no "happy love", as Louis Aragon says in a poem. To bear this pain of friendship and to experience unique happiness in it, is not only permitted, but demanded by our Christian life. Friendship is an essential precondition of true life and true vitality.

In his celebrated "Rules of Choice" Ignatius of Loyola gives us a most valuable piece of advice on how to make decisions in the important situations of our life. He says in his *Exercises*: I should imagine a man whom I have never seen or known and wish him every attainable perfection. Then I should weigh up what I should say to him that he should do or choose to the greater glory of God, our Lord and to the greater perfection of his soul. And in this way I am to act myself and keep to the rule that I have made for others (No. 185).

Here Ignatius is appealing to a very deep motive of the human heart, to the selfless feeling for another being. But we have at some time denied this pure prompting of friendship and of friendliness towards almost every being whom we have met in our life. We have in some respect betrayed every friend, we have perhaps wished him evil, not helped him in his troubles. *Vice versa*: Perhaps we have betrayed him by holding on to him in a too obvious way, by not letting him go, by clinging to him, that is, by wanting to be in some way to him God, that is, that without which he cannot exist.

Ignatius knows very well that we are not truly a friend of our friends—into the innermost and hiddenmost part of our heart. This is why he advises us to enter upon a "pure friendship", that is, to imagine someone who is completely unknown to us, someone we have never seen, a man who combines in himself as it were the features of the whole of humanity, and to wish him all possible perfection. In this way the whole sympathy with being that is hidden in our heart can emerge, the unqualified affirmation of another person. In this mood we should consider what we would say to this man if he had to make a decision in our situation. This advice speaks of a very great wisdom and profound knowledge of the human heart. Often a man who is uncertain in everything that concerns himself and who does not know which way to turn can often say to others with remarkable clarity what they have to do. In this lies a special grace of God: the grace to be grace for others. There is more than psychology in this direction of Ignatius. We find in it potentially a whole theology, even teaching concerning the grace of human friendship, which perhaps even points the way for the future of humanity.

6. LOVE

In this section let us meditate on the most fundamental Christian attitude to the world: the attitude of love. Today the word has become alarmingly ambiguous—perhaps this was the case in every age. It is possible to write high-sounding words about love, but what it is in its essence will only be understood by one who has already experienced love. What is a life that is lived genuinely, from the roots? It is a life of love.

Let us attempt to give a picture that is both faithful and enthusiastic of that reality that we call love, love which comes upon us like destiny, that we feel within ourselves like an incomprehensible and yet inwardly obvious power. It rises from the depth of the unconscious. It is like an inner necessity, a compulsion that, if we feel it, takes us over completely. If we love we can do nothing but love. Love works in us with a momentum of its own and almost hurts us. "I am sick from love," says the bride in the Song of Songs. Love can also become a disastrous catastrophe in our lives. A man must learn how to love, how to control this excitement of his whole being which rises from his soul. He cannot let every loving impulse grow aimlessly and senselessly, but must shape and bind it, give it fulfilment or refuse it this fulfilment. Thus genuine and mature love is a "virtue", that is, an attitude to the world that has to be learnt by effort. If we do not really "learn" it, then love can bring us boundless suffering. It is a strange thing that we "have to" love and at the same time "learn" this love with pain and suffering. The mere "feeling" of love can inflame a man of demonic violence.

It would be better in our meditation on love to be sparing of high-sounding words. Delicate things have to be handled delicately. In Western literature there is no text (perhaps with the exception of the "Reflection on the Attainment of

Love" of St Ignatius of Loyola) that speaks more essentially about love as an attitude that has to be "acquired" than the thirteenth chapter of St Paul's first letter to the Corinthians. Let us consider this text meditatively (and not exegetically) and try to see what it has to offer us for our lives. It is perhaps the most compressed and important expression of the Christian attitude in the world. St Paul says:

> If I speak in the tongues of men and of angels, but have not love, I am a noisy gong or a clanging cymbal. And if I have prophetic powers, and understand all mysteries and all knowledge, and if I have all faith so as to remove mountains, but have not love, I am nothing. If I give away all I have, and if I deliver my body to be burnt, but have not love, I gain nothing. Love is patient and kind; love is not jealous or boastful; it is not arrogant or rude. Love does not insist on its own way; it is not irritable or resentful; it does not rejoice at wrong, but rejoices in the right. Love bears all things, believes all things, hopes all things, endures all things.
>
> Love never ends; as for prophecies, they will pass away; as for tongues, they will cease; as for knowledge, it will pass away. For our knowledge is imperfect and our prophecy is imperfect; but when the perfect comes, the imperfect will pass away. When I was a child, I spoke like a child, I thought like a child, I reasoned like a child; when I became a man, I gave up childish ways. For now we see in a mirror dimly, but then face to face. Now I know in part; then I shall understand fully, even as I have been fully understood. So faith, hope, love abide, these three; but the greatest of these is love (1 Cor. 13. 1–13).

This astonishing text, whose anthropological and philosophical content we now wish to consider, is a strange stringing-together and mixture of statements, definitions, antitheses and pieces of interpretation. When we examine it more closely, however, we shall see that it is not possible to speak of love in any other way. The extraordinary thing is that Paul is not attempting in any way to define love itself. He distinguishes it from the other virtues and gifts: he enumerates its qualities, he circles round it. But this already contains an important statement: it is impossible to speak about love; one has to have experienced it; one must be shattered by it. Love is a primary experience. But it is impossible to lay hold on a primary experience; we cannot and must not pull it to pieces with words. The essential always eludes our intellectual efforts and our language. It is given only as an experience.

Love is everything

If I speak in the tongues of men and angels, but have not love, I am a noisy gong or a clanging cymbal. We do not want to investigate here in detail what Paul wanted to say to the community of Corinth, but rather what he himself had experienced. Obviously there were in Corinth men "endowed with the spirit", who had pressed forward to the uttermost frontier of what can be experienced by human beings and were able, stammering and stuttering, to bring back the inexpressible into the sphere of the expressible. The historical and psychological details of this "speaking with tongues" are unimportant here. The important thing for us is the basic experience, namely: although you may speak as beautifully as is possible for a man, even if you speak like an angel—if you do not have love, then it is all so much "old iron". You have not done nor have you experienced the essential thing. Your talking sounds good, it even moves men's hearts, it shatters them. But what is behind it? Nothing. Sheer emptiness. You pronounce words that do not express the essential thing. Your language, your delivery is moving, exciting, even illuminating—it is simply splendid. But you yourself are not behind it. And thus your language becomes meaningless, thin. It has a saddening effect. You are seeking only yourself, you want to make an impression. If you have never loved, how can you dare to speak about essentials? Your words will die away. They are an enjoyment of yourself and a magnificent display of yourself. Prove first that you place the other person above the interest of your own existence, that you want to spare the other person all that our world can inflict in the way of cares, suffering and wounds. First protect the other person, against himself, if it must be. Struggle for another, protect him, give him life and inner growth. Hence, for Paul, love is service. Our words are, however, always hollow and empty. We must first prove existentially that our words are honest. It is easy to fool others. Even the meatiest speeches are of no use if love is not behind them. Love communicates itself quite quietly, through simple assistance and faithfully staying with someone. Anyone can make beautiful speeches. The real "language" of love, however, sounds quite different. It is a giving of one's self and not an emotional eruption, nor is it an intelligent explanation.

And if I have prophetic powers, and understand all mysteries and all knowledge, and if I have all faith, so as to move mountains, but have not love, I have nothing. Here is a new, even more impressive distinction. A prophet is a man who is able to interpret the events of the world in terms of the grace of God. A man "understands all mysteries" if he is able to stand in amazement before the inexplicable and grasp it with the whole sensibility of his being, with a penetration that constantly grows and reaches into hidden truths. A man "believes" when—perhaps still inwardly doubtful—he exposes himself to a reality that cannot be constructed from the stuff of our world; when he is taken over to the roots of his existence by the other, by an absolute—which he cannot explain; when through this inner power of being addressed and laid hold of, he can sometimes even do things that amaze others and even the cosmic law; who can "move mountains".

In these three qualities we are given a striking picture of human life: prophetic, knowing and believing life. Anthropologically, a dynamic that embraces the whole being of man on the basis of the essential, towards which it is moving. And even here Paul says: No. All this is not really true. Not prophecy, not knowledge, and not faith, although they are important, beautiful and indispensable; none of these is the ultimate basis, but love.

What is this love to which Paul accords such precedence? The more intensively Paul makes the distinction from other "gifts of the spirit", the clearer it becomes that we are nothing if we do not love.

If I give away all I have, and if I deliver my body to be burnt, but have not love, I gain nothing. Karl Barth says about this passage: "There is in fact a love that is without love, a devotion that is no devotion; a paroxysm of self-love which has wholly the form of a love of God and one's brother that is genuine and knows no limits, which is not, however, concerned at all with God and one's brother. . . . Love alone counts—not deeds of love as such, not even the greatest. They could also be performed without love and then are meaningless—even more: they are then done against God and against one's brother."

If love was described before as service, then here "selflessness" is added as an essential element of love. Even in so-called "love" one can seek oneself. But one can also lose one's love in apparently unselfish action. A strange quality of love emerges here: not caring about oneself, not looking back at oneself, having no intentions. One can give up everything, even one's own life, but unless it is done absolutely for nothing, then it is nothing.

Here we have reached the outermost frontier of the humanly expressible. Perhaps true love consists simply in what the comforting psalm verse says: "I have become a beast of burden before your countenance, I have become a nothing . . .". This not caring about oneself, this purity of self-sacrifice, this not wanting anything from the other person, this accepting of the being of another, just as it is, is what love is: without this basic selflessness we are nothing, however many deeds of love we may perform. We are not loving, but seek only our own selves. Any man who has loved understands this: even through kindness one can put the other person in the wrong; through devotion one can even "offend"

others. As long as love is not detached from one's own self,
it is not love.

The argument of this astonishing text is remorseless, but
it is also constructive. It reveals to us the true dimensions of
humanity. Curiously, Paul continues in an unexpected direction. He describes, now positively, now negatively, the qualities of this attitude of man, which he previously said that he
could not speak about.

The qualities of love

The description of love in Paul is very fragmentary. We
can see that this man has experienced the real nature of love;
this is just the reason why he cannot speak about it. The argument does not come so much from his brain, but from his
heart. Thus it has a strange logic that only the heart can
understand. The experience, which vibrates in itself, releases
fragments of thought, intuitive insights, each of which, however, strikes right to the heart of the matter.

Love is patient. Now Paul begins to express his experience of love positively. The description begins with an undramatic quality which is, nevertheless, a life-supporting one:
with patience. It means that a man can stay with another for
a long time, even till death; that he supports the other but
not in a casual and indifferent way, but in creative faithfulness. It is the courage to support the other, to help him to
carry his own existence; the courage to live fully in time and
to show genuine devotion to the loved being in a way that is
always new and always different; the courage not to cut
through the thread of love, but to prove through a lived presence that the other can depend in all situations of life on our
staying with him.

Without this courage for a long devotion, sustained faithfully, the close life of men together can become a hell. Self-
education to a faithfulness that is ready for renunciation, not
capitulating before the task of persisting, the slow overcoming
of differences, the control of the inconstancy of our urges is

part of the essential nature of true love and true humanity. In this view love is an unconditional being there for the other person.

(*Love is*) *kind; love is not jealous or boastful.* This quiet and humble patience that is open to every situation of life should be infused by a friendliness that appears in Scripture as "meekness". It is the quiet serenity of being with someone, though faced with the threat of so much haste, nerviness and discontent; the quiet acceptance of the mistakes and the vacillations of the other person, of his failures, of his inner unrest, of his physical and mental inadequacies; the quiet sparing of the other person by being considerate, polite, and sympathetically sharing his troubles.

This kind of love is not "jealous", it does not seek the recognition it deserves, it does not fight other people, it has no enemy. It does not seek to put others in the wrong and does not keep a catalogue of human shortcomings; it does not work itself into that unhealthy and life-destroying disillusionment about other people that is simply self-righteousness.

This kind and unjealous love is not "boastful". It does not press itself forward, it listens, even when the other person talks "rubbish" and does not put one's own self in the centre of admiration or pity.

We can now see how simple, luminous and clear that love is of which Paul speaks; but also how much daily and hourly effort and self-conquest it requires. It is the small, often unnoticed even automatic things from which the profoundest attitude to being grows. But the automatic things are by no means so automatic when one tries to perform them honestly in everyday life.

(*Love*) *is not arrogant or rude. Love does not insist on its own way.* Now Paul approaches the subject from another angle. He wants to show the form of genuine and mature love in the concave mirror of negatives. It is strange, the way he lists these negatives. First he says that love is not "arrogant". Obviously he means by this an important quality of love, but one that is very difficult to express in words, although the image of being "blown up" expresses it directly. It means a man who does not make himself greater than he really is; who does not take into himself anything hollow and empty; who does not over-estimate his own self, his concerns, his efforts and his significance. True love does not fill the sphere of life with its own being, but rather draws back, leaving life space in which to move freely, in which to flourish. It does not take into itself the insignificant, but lets the being of the other person stream into it, his vitality, his feelings, his joy, his thoughts, his individual existence. Only someone who can receive the present of the other being into himself truly loves. The self that constantly emphasizes itself is "blown up"; it forces others out of the sphere of being. Love, on the other hand, means restraint, inner detachment, not emphasizing oneself. Love "makes itself small", it looks away from itself, it is happy to see others enjoying what it perhaps lacks itself, perhaps it even rejoices that the other is greater.

The sincerity of love is shown in the fact that it is not "rude". The word is not meant here in the moralizing way; it refers to an inner event: the sensitivity of the lover. In love one does not behave like a boor, because one is so held by the being of the loved person that one has to be courteous towards it, from an inner compulsion. The decline of love is mirrored directly in the decline of manners. Love, on the other hand, has something aristocratic about it. It recognizes the good in the other person and lets him feel that he is valued and respected. It moderates the violence inborn in man, it seeks to ward off disagreeable things in order to spare the other person misfortune and unhappiness. This attitude consists simply in making life possible for others, smoothing over painful situations, considering the inner vulnerability of the other person, which is to acknowledge their dignity.

From this follows the chief characteristic of love. "Love does not insist on its own way". But this is infinitely difficult. It is so humiliating to be the person we are. Always the same, always this meanness of our own life. We would like to get on, often at the cost of the other person. We feel disappointed by everyone and alienated from our own selves. This is a danger, and a grave one, which threatens the very nature of love. It is the temptation to use other men in order to confirm ourselves, to enrich us.

How is it possible for a man to overcome this urge? Here again we have reached the limit of what can be described. The answer is, I believe, by loving. This is the mystery of love, that element of the detachment from oneself and the turning to others that cannot be investigated. It is the nature of love that this dark temptation which "aims at overcoming love in the loving person is effortlessly overcome by it" (Karl Barth). In loving, love simply cannot seek itself. It is incapable of it.

Now Paul's argument takes a sharp turn. He describes the victorious superiority of love, the victory of love in everyday life.

(Love) *is not irritable or resentful; it does not rejoice at wrong, but rejoices in the right.* An essential characteristic of love is a detachment of one's whole life; we do not get fed up with the other being, it does not easily get on our nerves. Thus love pushes no one into an attitude of opposition, it overcomes irritability totally.

This conquest is shown primarily in the fact that it is not "resentful", that it does not keep an account of the failures of the other person, that it does not bear ill-will to the loved one for the evil that he undoubtedly contains. True love simply cannot speak the absolutely perverse words that one so often hears: "I have forgiven you, but I have not forgotten." In his second letter to the Corinthians Paul takes up the same idea again: "All this is from God, who through Christ reconciled us to himself and gave us the ministry of reconciliation; that is, God was in Christ reconciling the world to himself, not counting their trespasses against them, and entrusting to us the message of reconciliation" (2 Cor. 5. 18–19). Bearing grudges can transform even the most beloved being in time into a monster, into a thing that one can no longer endure. It is part of the nature of love that it does not add up, that it does not keep an account.

This relaxed attitude of love has nothing in common with that attitude that "rejoices at wrong", with that inner vulgarity that sees with satisfaction that the other person has made a mistake, that he has failed in something, that he has really made a fool of himself. In this kind of life the essence of love disintegrates. From this it is only a small step to pride, to the monstrous statement that a man dares to say before his God who had himself crucified and despised for us: "Lord, I thank you that I am not as other men: like these robbers, deceivers, burglars, or even like this publican."

As against this, Paul says of the lover that he "rejoices in the right". This is joy in the luminous quality of the other's life, a profound well-wishing. I rejoice that the other has reached a higher degree of consciousness, of freedom, perhaps also of success in the world, of selflessness and devotion. It is that attitude in which God stands against us, from one creation of the world to all eternity. John has expressed it in a few words, but words that contain the essence of Christianity: "God is greater than our hearts" (1 John 3. 20).

Mature love

The demands that Paul has made are so high that he suddenly realizes that this love is probably unattainable by human beings. We must be patient with ourselves. If we want to love, we must constantly begin anew, in constantly fresh initiative and freedom, in persisting and enduring in what remains for us to do and in which we constantly fail. In four sections Paul now sketches this maturing process of love. True growth always takes place slowly. Patience—in its existentially realized form—is the growing man who understands himself and his relations to others correctly.

Love bears all things, believes all things, hopes all things, endures all things.   First we have four simple ideas: bearing, believing, hoping and enduring. When we love, how often we are exploited. We are unprotected, we lose, as it were, our own separate being, we feel that we are a plaything. The other person possibly treats love too lightly. Love must bear this disappointment and endure it in faith and hope. Often we are so tired; we would simply like to stop. We no longer believe the other person because we feel and perhaps have good proof that we are deceived. We no longer hope for a real change. This love cannot go on for ever!

But if we are honest, we must also look at the situation from the other side. It is true that there are circumstances in which we see that love, supposed love, has not become a sharing of lives. Then we ought to leave it alone. But if we have entered into a bond that is perhaps painful, then the only thing is bearing, believing, hoping and enduring. What would become of our world if no one were able to stay with anyone else?

In these four qualities of mature love Paul is basically describing only *one* attitude: through my selfless love I make it possible for the other person to love; I let him feel when I am with him that he is quite secure with me, that he can be wholly the person he is or would like to be; that my being does not limit him; that I do not reproach him for being what he is; that I can see in him the person that he will become. Perhaps new possibilities will awake in him—not at once perhaps, but in the course of the constant encounters he has. In this way I arouse him to find his human authenticity.

Love never ends. As for prophecies, they will pass away; as for tongues, they will cease; as for knowledge, it will pass. Paul returns here to his original idea—but as if in a spiral, on a higher level. What we hold in our hands at the end of our life is not our achievements and gifts. What builds up our real and everlasting life is the bearing of the burden of love, and nothing else. Everything that we have known, everything that has moved us, everything that we could express and formulate (the whole sphere of our domination and mastery of the world, the whole area of our achievements) will disappear one day in a transformation. Only love has radical continuity. This alone do we take untransformed and unbroken into the eternal fulfilment. Love is the "straight line"; it is the presence of the already fulfilled promise. This is expressed by Paul even more fully in his next words, which completely relativize all our successes:

For our knowledge is imperfect and our prophecy is imperfect; but when the perfect comes the imperfect will pass away. We cannot really perfect anything in our lives. Our longing, our awareness, our will are always reaching out; the realization always remains behind. The only thing that lasts is love. Everything else can be achieved only imperfectly. What seemed so clear and obvious to us years ago, or even months, suddenly proves to be wretched and empty. Not simply worthless but imperfect.

It is true that an intensely lived life grows in depth. We feel the desire for quietness, for stopping, for gathering ourselves. But this quietness has to be learnt, otherwise something in us is stunted. Otherwise we remain caught up in this whirl of fragmentary thoughts, in the unrest of desiring and anxiety. We must practise quiet lingering over a serious question, over an important thought. Only then do we acquire inwardness and depth. When silence is developed into a way of life, then something like wisdom and quiet understanding can emerge in our lives. This is, fundamentally, nothing but love. But it remains. True unity of life, holding together the differences, the distinctions, the contradictions and contrasts that weigh down our thinking and our language, and also the growth in union with our friends, with nature and also with our own lives—only love can achieve all this. Otherwise we ourselves remain imperfect: alien beings in an alien world. That is why Paul says:

When I was a child, I spoke like a child, I thought like a child, I reasoned like a child; when I became a man, I gave up childish ways. Paul is not speaking here against that great quality of being childlike that is praised in the gospels, that is that simplicity and directness of mind, the capacity of desireless awareness of another person, which are qualities of human authenticity that are difficult to acquire. But he is speaking against the childishness that does not want to mature, that constantly holds on to the provisional. We call a child childlike: but an adult who plays his way through life, who cannot work his way through to the seriousness of accepting responsibility and a task, we call childish.

This irresponsible, childish quality of thinking, speaking and judging bars our way to true love, for love brings, as we have said, a curious gravity, indeed often a threat of suffering into our lives. We have to "endure" in love. We cannot play with it or treat it irresponsibly. In exposing ourselves to the care, seriousness and the wearing away of love our life ripens towards what is essential. Only in this way and to this degree does "birth" take place in our lives.

But towards what future is this birth of man that takes place in love directed? Paul speaks of this in the fourth part of this highly packed text.

The future of love

What is the promise of the life that has matured in love? Paul expresses it in three sentences:

For now we see in a mirror dimly, but then face to face. Paul speaks of our fragmentary vision that is always "the wrong way round" (a mirror image)—as in all mirrors—and (he is speaking of an ancient mirror, which was simply finely polished metal) reflects the features in a blurred way. We experience reality in the alien medium of images and ideas; it is not yet given as an experience of one person to another. At bottom we experience almost everything "the wrong way round": God is very near to us, and we think he is a long way off; God is a long way off and we think he is very near. This mode of existence will be wholly transformed. God will become wholly a person for us, from face to face; direct, immediate, in a mutual seeing and touching. In the measure that I love, that will take place between me and God of which friends and lovers have a faint sense in the highest moments of their awareness of each other: I am you, and you are I. Love develops into an absolute perfection. This means:

Now I know in part; then I shall understand fully, even as I have been fully understood. This insignificant sentence contains the fullness of the promise of our earthly love. We shall know God, even as he knows us. This means that we shall go into the directness of his vision and his presence. We shall remain creatures, but with every fibre of our existence we will understand God in the way that he understands us. This means basically that we will become God. The fundamental dynamic of my earthly existence develops into a growth towards the infinite. And that is why Paul says finally:

So faith, hope, love abide, these three; but the greatest of these is love. Even in this eternal mutuality of God and his creature faith and hope will be preserved. Of course they will be changed into a direct relationship with God, transformed into sight, but nevertheless real. Faith remains: a constant standing over against God and receiving him in love; hope remains: the capacity and desire to receive still more from eternal love. These two must, of course, change their earthly form. They will not be perfected in our earthly obscurity and wanderings, but as a luminous, glowing, ever more beatific growth into an ever-growing God.

Irenæus of Lyons interprets this passage in Paul in the following way: "God must always be the greater. And not only in this world, but also in eternity. Thus God remains always the teacher, and man always the learner. Does not the apostle say that when everything else has passed away, these three alone will still remain: Faith, hope and love. For our faith in our teacher will remain forever unshaken, and we may hope to receive something more from God . . . Simply because he is good and possesses inexhaustible riches and a kingdom without end."

But love is the greatest. Why? Because it, and it alone, can pass into perfection without changing its form. Our faith and our hope are part of the fragmentary; they remain eternal, but they must assume an essentially new form: the form of sure, quiet, but—because God is infinite—eternal movement into God. Only love remains what it is—if it is, and by being, really love. But this means that it can and must already now be seen as an anticipation of the ultimate: the presence of heaven in our earthly life.

7. MAGNANIMITY

We have all experienced in different ways that our life is great, that it is moving towards the improbable and the unattainable: that our being is far greater than our actual existence. We have seen that if a man wants to continue in his humanity, he must constantly grow beyond his own limitations, he must constantly begin anew, he must expose himself to the claim and the challenge of something greater than himself. The fullness of what he senses is possible, is more than simply a concrete imitation. Total self-transcendence, the apprehension of the incomprehensible: this is the paradox of human life. Man can exist in his humanity only in an openness, in an orientation towards the absolute. We have all had this experience. But it is not enough to have experienced it. The man who lives authentically lives constantly from this experience. A life that has the courage to face constantly the challenge of something greater realizes what the ancients called the virtue of *magnanimitas*: magnanimity.

What is a man like who really fulfils the greatness of his life? He would not measure himself by the externals of his life, of his concretely realized destiny. His soul would be filled by an expanse of feeling and sensibility. Honours would not impress him. He would say to himself: no praise and recognition can really praise and recognize what I am in my innermost being. Misfortune and insults, the blows of fate, would not touch him in the centre of his being. They always miss the reality of the person. What he would really measure himself by would be his longing, that is, the most inward and hidden drive of life towards authentic greatness. His life would be glowing. There would be something at work in him that Thomas Aquinas describes by the strange phrase "*opinio vehemens*": an exaltedness, penetration and intense power of sensibility. He would accompany his life, his encounters, and the various events of his existence, everything that happened to him, with his whole mind; he would be really present. Not tensely, but with a calm and relaxed assurance, as well as an all-pervading fearlessness.

These three things, calmness, serenity and fearlessness are, according to medieval theology, the three components of magnanimity. The latter, then, is simply the hidden *élan* of a soul who seeks greatness in all the situations of life, which does not let itself be imprisoned by anything, but always sees and finds ways out.

If everything that we have tried to indicate here in brief outline were realized in a man as a constant attitude to being, then we would speak of the virtue of magnanimity, or, to express it better, of a courage for greatness.[5] In this kind of life the unusual would happen. It would not be an everyday life, not a part of the mass. This kind of man would have to suffer a lot: the tops of the highest trees are the most pulled about by the wind. The greatest have to face the storms. At the same time he would have a luminous simplicity—even in his language. He would be able to speak the greatest truths with the words of a child. Is it not astonishing that the great reformers of Carmel, John of the Cross and Teresa of Avila, when speaking of the austerity and the suffering of the mystical experience said it in poems and songs that were about love and flowers! And in this generous attitude to being there would be no arrogance. Such a man would regard his actual greatness as an undeserved gift. It is one of the great laws of being truly a person and is confirmed in the Gospel: it is the most humble creature who can be sure of having a most splendid destiny before it—so much so that it is able to say the whole *Magnificat* with plain obviousness and simplicity.

What prevents us from realizing this happy detachment of soul, this generosity of feeling, of living, of thinking and of the commitment of our life in our everyday living? The spiritual authors of the monastic life point out two dangers to

[5] A play on "Grossmut", "magnanimity", lit. "great mind". "Mut" in modern German means "courage".—Trans.

us, two conditions of the spirit that throw a man back on himself and his narrow world: sloth and anxiety.

Sloth

For the classical writers of the monastic life (e.g., Cassian or Bernard of Clairvaux) sloth (*acedia*), one of the seven deadly sins, has nothing to do with idleness or laziness, against which our schoolmasters, our fathers, or the solid citizens of the commercial world have constantly warned us. Its opposite is not industry and hard work, but magnanimity or high-mindedness (*magnanimitas*). Sloth is not a sin of youth. It is the noon-day devil, a temptation that befalls a man in the middle of his life, in the situation when he has to decide on a "second conversion". It is a temptation of the spirit that has been disillusioned by life, so much so, that its full significance was recognized first among educated men, in the cells of the monks. St Bonaventure even points out that it is so sublime and unique that those who live in the world can hardly understand it and have no name for it. It consists of a strange sadness, in a discouragement before greatness of soul, in a flight of the spirit from itself. This kind of man no longer finds pleasure in anything. He would like to depart from the centre of his own being and break out into activity—into the world of busy achievement, into the jungle of insignificant things. It is that heavy sadness of heart that no longer desires or is able to expect greatness of itself. It is a flight from oneself, an antipathy and boredom in the face of the great, the despair of a burnt-out inside, the inner desolation of weakness.

This flight from the essential is seen in a wandering restlessness of mind; in a garrulousness of speech; in an insatiability of curiosity; in lack of discipline in the area of what can be seen, heard and experienced; in inner restlessness; in the variety of ideas and images which pour through the mind; in inconstancy of place and decision; in indifference; in smallness of mind; in a strange lack of goodwill towards others and a constant resentment and criticism of everything that attacks our own being.

We have compiled this list on the basis of the analyses of Gregory the Great, Cassian and Thomas Aquinas. It contains practically all the symptoms of what Kierkegaard in his *Sickness unto Death*, describes as the "despair of weakness", and what Heidegger describes in his *Being and Time* as "everyday living": the joyless, irritable and narrowly selfish renunciation of greatness.

We have found a hint in Gregory the Great of how we can overcome this spiritual joylessness and paralysis of the soul's flight. He says: "The sin of spiritual sloth, of the soul's joylessness can be overcome by a man's constantly thinking of the goods of heaven. A spirit which takes to light in the happiness of the expectation of such joyful things cannot possibly feel discouraged."

This injunction contains more than just a pious exhortation. It expresses the essential attitude of Christian living: the Christian lives his life, as it were, from heaven. The so-called "last things" are, in reality, the "first". A man should try to understand himself essentially in terms of his final perfection. What takes place in Christian living is basically only a "being born". The Christian—by being a Christian, and in so far as he is one—lives towards a radical otherness, a transcendent greatness, an unsurpassable future that is called heaven. That is why a taste for happiness, confidence and joy in greatness are not just an additional part of Christianity; they determine the whole Christian reality: as the orientation and view forward, as the key in which everything in it is tuned, as the dawn of an expected day. Christ is a man only if he proved to his fellow men by his own lived and constantly practised behaviour that life is still growing within us; God has prepared for us eternal joy; we are moving towards a state of endless and unbroken life.

To be a Christian, then, means to give testimony by having relaxed detachment and a joyful orientation towards what is great, in every situation, even the most difficult. As Christians we simply have not time to be sad, dispirited and depressed, to be satisfied with our achievements and to forget hope. We have so little time, and there is so much for which we can and must hope.

This demands of us a faithfulness to hope, an endurance in expectation. This is how we should measure our Christianity, our Christian testimony in the present time. We have no use today for tired, blasé and satiated Christians. The future is a central problem for the man of today. He senses that he is, biologically and intellectually, only at the beginning of his development. The best proof of the truth of Christianity today would be to testify by our thinking and our life that Christianity is the religion of radical hope, that Christians form the actual germ of a new humanity and that, *vice versa*, where Christianity is fully hoped for, it already finds its realization—perhaps under strange and unrecognized forms, but none the less real.

Anxiety

Anxiety is one of the phenomena of our inner life that is hardest to describe and at the same time is one of the most universal. Since it pervades the lives of all of us, and is, in fact, our gravest suffering, we must proceed in our analysis with great reserve. It is easy to entertain men when they are happy; but it is difficult to say or write even a few words that can support them in difficult hours. And the hours of anxiety are among the heaviest of our life.

They are heavy because they are narrowing for us. Anxiety is derived from the Latin word *"angustus"* ("narrow"). The experience of narrowness is essential for the mood of anxiety. Man experiences himself as narrowed even in the womb. As a little child he is a completely helpless creature who would perish if the loving care in the bosom of the family were withdrawn from him. From his evolutionary origin man preserves the dark memories of the struggles and tribulations to which life was exposed in its long and complex growth. His individual psychological structure along a line of development commits him more and more to specific kinds of behaviour, reaction, feeling and decision. Sooner or later the time comes when he has to step himself into the battlefield of life, accept responsibility and deal with the difficult problems of living.

From all these internal and external influences his destiny emerges, something that has grown and is uncontrollable, a course of life. The breadth of his spirit becomes narrowed down, and only through this does it become possible for him to have an individual destiny. His thinking becomes bound to customary ways of thought. His decisions are largely dictated by external necessities and by previous historically and culturally conditioned decisions. His feelings generally follow the lines prescribed and followed by the spirit of the time.

All this disturbs a man. He suspects that behind it there is something deeper, something more fundamental. He imagines that he is the plaything of forces that are not part of his own being. And this is in fact the case. He is at the mercy of alien powers of which he is afraid. This fear, which is often called "objective anxiety", is a feeling which lurks in the depths of man. It accompanies the growth of the human individual in all his phases. Its concrete, visible, and therefore not totally threatening phenomena are simple particular points of concentration: in them emerges what lies hidden in the depth of man: an "unobjective anxiety", which is no longer an anxiety of something, but anxiety itself. In it man is touched in his most personal centre by something that he cannot further define or localize and to which he cannot, for that reason, respond with a clear attitude.

In this unobjective anxiety man experiences himself as fundamentally threatened, into the last dimension of his being. What threatens him is not a part of a world of objects. The threat is everywhere. Everything is bathed in it. Everywhere, where concrete, objective and thematically stateable anxiety is experienced, there arises out of the depth of man something "groundless" and inexplicable, something paralysing and annihilating, a narrowing of the human being that is given from the very beginning.

Language reaches here the bounds of its possibilities. Death, sickness, rejection of love, its possible and necessary "loss", and everything else that can be called an object of anxiety, are not the same thing as this profound experience: one's whole being is made unreal, it becomes uncanny, one is no longer at home in it[6]; it is, as it were, no longer fit for human habitation. The space in which we live becomes distorted, and the inner structure of the person collapses. Our whole humanity falls into a boundless confusion. Images of primaeval anxiety rise up from our soul and surprise us at night and during the day. Terrifying pictures scatter our individual thoughts and feelings. Ghosts with distorted faces appear, just for a moment, in a frightful flashing light. Our own despair is what we really suffer, because we can do nothing to help ourselves.

In the seventeenth chapter of the Book of Wisdom the night of the liberation of Israel is described in a way that we would call today an interpretation in terms of existential psychology. Egypt is overcome by anxiety. It is a night of impotence. The words are:

Throughout the night, which was really powerless, and which beset them from the recesses of powerless Hades, they all slept the same sleep, and now were driven by monstrous spectres, and now were paralyzed by their souls' surrender, for sudden and unexpected fear overwhelmed them. And whoever was there fell down, and thus was kept shut up in a prison not made of iron; for whether he was a farmer or a shepherd or a workman who toiled in the wilderness, he was seized, and endured the inescapable fate; for with one train of darkness they all were bound. Whether there came a whistling wind, or a melodious sound of birds in wide-spreading branches, or the rhythm of violently rushing water, or the harsh crash of rocks hurled down, or the unseen running of leaping animals, or the sound of the most savage roaring beasts, or an echo thrown back from a hollow of the mountains, it paralyzed them with terror. For the whole world was illumined with bril-

[6] By hyphenating "un-heimlich", "uncanny", the author gives to the word the force of the above phrase.—Trans.

liant light, and was engaged in unhindered work, while over those men alone heavy night was spread, an image of the darkness that was destined to receive them; but still heavier than darkness were they to themselves. But for the holy ones there was very great light.

In this description there emerges a picture of total anxiety. A cosmos of anxiety is described, a world that is totally formed from anxiety, in which everything is a function of anxiety. This world is uninhabitable, the air in it cannot be breathed. Since the threat remained anonymous, man cannot protect himself against it. A bewildering narrowness arises. There is no dependence on anything. No thought and no reflection can help one out of this condition.

We do not intend to consider here whether this total confusion of our life comes from guilt, from psychological or other reasons which depth-psychology seeks to explain. Ultimately all that is unimportant. We have to live the life that has been accorded us by the grace of God, whether it has elements of guilt and morbidity in it or not. And this life is largely influenced by the powers of sloth and anxiety. This and no other existence is the place in which we experience the absolute, the chosen place of salvation for us. It is precisely anxiety that can lead us to the highest experience of the absolute. In it life is literally driven into a corner. When man experiences himself and his life as "cornered", as something that no longer has any inner support, he is able to experience —precisely in this—that he can live his life, if at all, only in God; in God, who is not part of the structures of this world, of the framework of his own psychic life. When he experiences meaninglessness and the self-torture of anxiety man has the desire to run away. Nothingness, that which annihilates him, presses upon him and creates in his soul a chaotic loss of relationships, a world that man cannot support; with the last power of his life he throws himself into the arms of God and places himself under the protection of being. In this way an experience that is in itself wholly negative can, at its

uttermost point, change into sheer positivity, into the experience of God.

Augustine, who experienced in his life the abysses of
despair, once tried to give an ultimate significance to extreme
meaninglessness. He said: "The man who, wandering in the
abyss, screams out overcomes the abyss. The scream itself
lifts him above the abyss." Let us consider this idea carefully.
It leads us into the centre of interpretation of Christian life.
Man is not dependent on himself, he has nothing beneath his
feet; the only thing he can hope for is God's mercy and faithfulness, the eternally incomprehensible mystery of his love.

Here the central idea of providence emerges. How can one
bring home to a man of today that profound experience of
devout souls that they call providence? Even today we would
have to say the important decisive thing quite briefly, in the
way that Philip was able to when talking with the treasurer
from Ethiopia. There are in the history of mankind "primal
words", in which the whole religious experience of the particular epoch is concentrated and which one only has to speak
in order to be immediately understood. In Scripture itself
and then in the course of the history of faith and salvation
we find a large number of such primal words, which always
refer to and imply the whole, but at the same time are the
particular approach of a period to the whole of the Christian
experience. Love, one's neighbour, brother, challenge, future,
hope, world, encounter, development—these are among the
keywords in which the one phase is still existentially realiza-
ble for men of today. Unfortunately the word providence is
not among them. And yet it cannot be removed from the
Christian's self-understanding. What is meant by the idea of
providence cannot be excluded from the Christian pictures
of God and man, especially today, in the age of satiety and
anxiety.

Men today protest against any injustice. But a "magic"
conception of providence would be unjust. Some people have
found the trick: they only need to say a word to their pal God
and they have fine weather for their trip. God is pressed into
practical service in everyday life, to give success and well-

being. This is exactly the definition of magic, and it is constantly condemned in Scripture as inspired by the self-seeking heart. God has expressly forbidden this view of providence in his revelation—the book of Job is about nothing else. It is simply not true that the man who succeeds in many things in life is a better person. There are pious men devoted to God who lead a wretched and unsuccessful life, encountering every misfortune, exposed to every despair and danger, finding themselves in difficult situations, everywhere in their life, always being just where lightning strikes. If providence were a means of earthly security and temporal well-being, then it would not be a truth revealed by God, that is, not a message of joy and liberation, but an injustice that cried to heaven. The good news of providence was not given to the successful, but to the oppressed, the anxious, the discouraged and the weary. To us all! It says: If you have nobody to help you; if you feel lost in the world; if your own weakness and the burden of your sins oppress you; if you really see no way out: then think of God. He is your friend. He is always with you and will always help you.

Accordingly, providence is nothing but what Paul calls "hope against hope", the last refuge of the oppressed and downtrodden. The others do not need providence. They have already provided enough for themselves. But when human strength is at an end, then only God can help. And this ultimate help of God that can always be depended on is called, simply, providence. It is the epitome of salvation. It means that the unfortunate are beloved of God, precisely because they are most dependent on his love. But the most unfortunate man is the sinner. It is him in particular whom God surrounds with his boundless benevolence, with his absolute goodness.

The essence of providence consists in this change of thinking. Not so much in imagining that God interferes in a miraculous way in our lives, removing dangers, preventing and annihilating the attacks of an unfriendly world. Providence is a transformation in grace of the whole human world of experience. It means that in every situation of our lives, in every perplexity there is always a way out. Everything can become a grace. Every situation of life, every suffering is already taken up into the all-embracing mercy of God. Perhaps everything will still remain the same. The threat does not depart; the child for whom I am praying dies; I must continue to bear my anxieties and try to cope in an alien and unfriendly world. But in all this and through all this God is still standing by me. His love—however incomprehensible it may seem to us—expresses itself in all that. If we understand this, then we are living in the providence of God. We can say to ourselves: it hurts terribly, but it does not really matter.

Already in the Old Testament there was a "deep current" in the understanding of salvation, especially in the prophetic books and in the wisdom literature. Isaiah always expresses a great comfort: "Fear not" (41. 10). "Fear not, for I have redeemed you" (43. 1). "Even though I walk through the valley of the shadow of death, I fear no evil; for thou art with me" (Ps. 22. 4). "The Lord is my light and my salvation; whom shall I fear? The Lord is the stronghold of my life; of whom shall I be afraid?" (Ps. 27. 1). "If you sit down, you will not be afraid; when you lie down, your sleep will be sweet. Do not be afraid of sudden panic" (Prov. 3. 24). "He who listens to me will dwell secure and will be at ease, without dread of evil" (Prov. 1. 33).

From these revelations of God, from his faithfulness and unshakable constancy in his loving concern there grows in the people of God a new, hitherto unknown dimension of the understanding of being, a serenity even in times of suffering, to which we shall devote a special section. We know very well—and this is most important for the understanding of the idea of providence—that God tested this people severely and did not avert from it the blows of fate. But within the world of its experience he always left a door open into the other, into a place removed from the suffering. The chief thing can be had by everyone under all circumstances. There are no proletarians of salvation. God's love upholds me in all the situations of my life.

This joy of liberation is expressed powerfully in the Letter to the Romans: "Who shall separate us from the love of Christ? Shall tribulation, or distress, or persecution, or famine, or nakedness, or peril, or sword? . . . I am sure that neither death, nor life, nor angels, nor principalities, nor things present, nor things to come, nor powers, nor height, nor depth, nor anything else in all creation, will be able to separate us from the love of God in Christ Jesus our Lord" (8. 35–39). The whole teaching of the New Testament on providence is summarized in this text: There is nothing in the world, no power, no sin, no guilt, no defect of character or psychology that could stop the breaking in of grace, that is, the love of God for us in Jesus Christ. Everything else is ultimately without significance. Confidence in ultimate salvation should be part of the Christian's life, the world of his concrete experience. Even against his own heart. Even against that which constantly accuses us, disturbs us and takes from us our courage. God himself demands of us that we should commune with our own heart. But before God. "We shall . . . reassure our hearts before him whenever our hearts condemn us; for God is greater than our hearts, and he knows everything" (1 John 3. 19–20).

The words of the Letter to the Romans penetrate still further into the mystery of providence: "In everything God works for good with those who love him" (8. 28). Absolutely everything. Augustine adds in his commentary—even our sins. For the Christian experience of providence it is not important what has taken place in our life, what we are at present and what can happen to us in the future (by our own fault or by someone else's). So long as we preserve the tiniest flicker of love for God, then everything is still open. Everything can still change its foreground meaning and can be a stage on the journey to God.

In all this we must keep our eyes fixed on one thing: the person who speaks here is Jesus Christ. In him the goodness and mercy of God appeared in our midst. From this person proceeded the final revelation. This is: "Behold, I have set before you an open door, which no one is able to shut" (Rev. 3. 8). These words are the essence of providence.

In this connection it may be said that the message of providence is basically a message of the resurrection of Christ. The apostles experienced the death of the man who in his life radiated nothing but understanding and goodness. At last there was someone who did not let himself be impressed by any power, who placed himself wholly beside the weak and oppressed. A simple man who was great primarily in that he entered into all the narrowness of life and even when beset by weariness always found a good word for his friends. He never hated, condemned no one, never returned evil with evil. He did not break the broken reed, nor extinguish the smoking wick. He was killed. There were men who could not tolerate such a purity of goodness. In their faith in the resurrection his friends realized that the mind of the saviour had absolute validity, whatever the world might think of it. This is one of the most important elements in the experience of the resurrection: goodness, love of one's fellow men, forgiveness and affection are the ultimate criteria of life. This man Jesus of Nazareth, with the attitude of life that he realized on earth, had become the sign of everything that was truly human. From now on everyone who honestly lived his own human reality realized the mind of Christ, and was therefore basically—explicitly or anonymously—a Christian. There is now no power on earth that can take Christ from us. Let those who have made their selfishness and ruthless self-assertion the law of their life cause us suffering and distress; in the profoundest region of our life they have no more power over us. In his resurrection Christ spoke his infinite "yes" to everything in the human heart that is meant honestly, to all mercy and forgiveness, to all goodness and hope: "In him it is always Yes. For all the promises of God find their Yes in him. That is why we utter the Amen through him" (2 Cor. 1. 20). The pettiness and envy of our world was finally conquered: "When he raised him from the dead and made him sit at his right hand in heavenly places, (he is) far above all rule and authority and power and dominion, and above every name that is named, not only in this age but also in that which is to come" (Eph. 1. 20–21).

We have seen that the essential element of human life is a drive towards greatness, a magnanimity of soul that has become an habitual attitude. It is constantly threatened in our life by spiritual satiety and uncontrollable anxiety. In Christ God has given us the chance of moving out of our narrow life into the broad expanse of absolute fulfilment. He has given us the capacity of breaking out from all the situations of our life and of always beginning again, of growing out beyond our own limitations and restrictions. But how can this happen concretely?

The point at which all the hopes of the human heart that are directed towards the absolute are concentrated is, according to the Christian Gospel, our brother. He who goes towards his brother encounters God. The conclusion from this fundamental thought is obvious: you find your real greatness only in serving your brother; in this you overcome the narrowness and the fears of your own life.

If we speak here of the love of our neighbour, we do not mean that achievement of social politics—however useful and important it might be—that the apostle speaks of: "If I give away all I have, and if I deliver my body to be burnt, but have not love, I gain nothing" (1 Cor. 13. 3). Here it is a question of revealing that secret that is hidden in the words of Christ: "You shall love the Lord your God with all your heart, and with all your soul, and with all your mind. This is the great and first commandment. And a second is like it, You shall love your neighbour as yourself. On these two commandments depend all the law and the prophets" (Matt. 22. 37–40).

According to the words of Christ the keeping of these two commandments, which he expressly likens to each other, means life: "Do this, and you will live" (Luke 10. 28). In Matthew, in the eschatological judgment discourses of Christ, the love of our neighbour appears as the only criterion according to which man is judged (25. 31–46). Paul describes the love of our neighbour as the fulfilment of the law (Rom. 13. 8) and hence as the bond of perfect harmony (Col. 3. 14). He even goes as far as equating faith and that wretched meanness of the daily round in which our life is worn away: "If

anyone does not provide for his relatives, and especially for
his own family, he has disowned the faith and is worse than
an unbeliever" (1 Tim. 5. 8). Could we not reverse the logic
of this sentence? It then turns into an offer of salvation that
is unexpectedly striking: "If someone provides for his relatives, and especially for his own family, he possesses the faith
and is a believer." In his hymn to love Paul presents the love
of one's brother as the Christian way of life (1 Cor. 13. 1–
13). In John this idea is taken to an unheard-of extreme:
God has loved us only in order that we should love one another (cf. 13. 34). This is the new commandment that could
not be given before and only became possible in the incarnation of God: "This is *my* commandment, that you love
one another as I have loved you" (John 15. 12). The important thing for him is obviously not that we shall expressly
know and love him. The love of our neighbour is sufficient.
He has not loved us in order that we shall love him back, but
that we should love one another: "Beloved, let us love one
another; for love is of God, and he who loves is born of God
and knows God. He who does not love does not know God;
for God is love. . . . If God so loved us, we also ought to
love one another" (1 John 4. 7–11).

To love God, once one has properly known him, is very
easy. To love our brother is difficult. And yet the second is the
criterion of the first: "He who does not love his brother whom
he has seen, cannot love God whom he has not seen" (1 John
4. 20). And the supreme sentence in which the essence of
Christianity is expressed: "If we love one another, God abides
in us" (1 John 4. 12). Why? Here we must think carefully.
Let us go back to an idea of Karl Rahner's:

Is love of our neighbour merely a commandment? Did God
arbitrarily equate human love with the love of him? Is our
neighbour simply material, an opportunity for the love of
God? This would be a disastrous misunderstanding. In loving
our neighbour we are loving God. The two are really, and not
just arbitrarily, one. The love of our neighbour is always a
movement towards God. In the love of another human being
the whole mystery of humanity is realized. It contains every-

thing that a man is and can still be: his infinite depth, his imperfectibility, his encounter with the mystery, his hope and despair, his venturing into the unknown, even his death.

Man has never seen God. We must take these words of revelation absolutely seriously. Man will never be able to see God, since the absolute mystery is humanly absolutely unknowable. Even in heaven he will see God as a mystery, as something from which he lives and into which he can move throughout eternity, loving and always knowing more. The only concrete way in which man can realize the absolute love of God is in loving his neighbour. The possibility of his becoming a self is absolutely dependent on the love of his neighbour. His neighbour is not a task that is committed to him from outside, but the condition of his becoming an I, of becoming and being a self, of possessing an existentially fulfilled authenticity. From these thoughts we can derive two statements that express our relationship to our neighbour and to God.

1. The love of our neighbour is the essential action of human existence.

The act of personal love towards another human being is the fundamental action of a human being, which includes everything else and gives it meaning, direction and measure. All other statements about man must be regarded as statements about his love for other people. Only through experiencing the personal Thou does a man really find himself; only in loving another person does a man know himself in his unique being, in his capacity to love and be loved. Everything else, every achievement and attainment in human life is not part of what constitutes our being. Only love, only that ultimate experience of being torn away from ourselves is able to lead us to that authenticity of being that cannot be reached through being centred on oneself. To be a self always means sacrifice. But the sacrifice is realized only when it is not measured in terms of self-enrichment, where it no longer counts and estimates, where even one's own life becomes unimportant: in love. This cannot be proved, but only seen, as it were, with the heart—but then with direct evidence. This insight is the fruit of practice.

If love takes such a central place in man's realization of his existence, then God can reach man only through the medium of the love of his neighbour. There is no other way for him, if he seeks to reach the sphere of human reality.

2. The love of one's neighbour is the only way in which we can experience God.

We have already indicated that God is given to us nowhere in experience, but can be sensed only as a longing for more, as a dissatisfaction with what we have already achieved, as the longing of a restless heart. This experience of radical unrest, however, can only be set off in us when our humanity becomes central and essential, in the love for another person. If the love of our neighbour contains the whole mystery of man's being, then it must also contain the profoundest part of all the mysteries of life: God. Only in love does man experience the very roots of his existence: the abysses of happiness, of failure and of hope. Only by love seeking to be nothing but the love of a finite other person, does it discover that from the beginning it signified more than what it had to offer, and what response of love it encountered. Thus all love of our neighbour, even in its darkest and most confused realization, is a saving event, a primary act of the love of God. The longest journey in life is the journey to a beloved person, because it never stops, but must be continued into eternity, into God, in order to develop all that is contained in it from the beginning as goal and potentiality.

It is not a question of loving our neighbour because God has commanded it, that is, it is not a means and a channel of our own salvation. This would not be love but selfishness. Our thoughts are in a directly opposite direction: it is precisely finite devotion, love that seeks nothing but warmth towards the finite, endangered and yet delightful other person; it is always a love of God; it includes the final fulfilment in heaven, and is a proof that God exists—and, still more, that this God has become man. Every lover experiences with a direct insight the reality of Christ, even if he has never heard of him. God has so sanctified love that ultimately nothing will remain of human life—even of Christian life, of faith, hope, the sacraments and the Church—than just this love, that gives us our only possibility of living in God, without end.

The only true greatness of man is founded in the love of our neighbour. The drive towards greatness, magnanimity, proves itself genuine and total only in the venture of self-sacrifice. By showing through our simple service for our brother that life has an unplumbable depth, we experience ourselves that our being reaches into equally unplumbable depths. This experience conquers our satiety and our anxiety. Only the man who has committed himself to giving new courage for life to a beloved person and to protecting it from the dangers of the world can experience that he bears within himself something that is liberated from all sloth and anxiety, the ultimate depth of being, that which places us above all other creatures. The magnanimity that is realized in the banality of everyday life, experienced only in the help and service of a beloved other person proves that—despite everything that we are and have done in our provisional, imperfect nature—we are really the culmination of the universe. We are more than angels. We are men who in the incarnate Christ have been drawn down into the depth of the Trinity.

Thomas Aquinas said once: "Men, who are in the state of being on the way, are of a higher rank than the angels. They have not yet reached a higher place than they, but through the power of love they have the strength to reach a higher degree of blessedness than the angels have. As if we were to say that the seed of a great tree is more powerful than a small tree, however much smaller the seed may look at the moment." We experience daily in bitter humiliation that we are not yet great. But the greatness to which we are called is boundless.

8. SERENITY

There are two kinds of thinking. Calculating thinking and reflective thinking. Both are, in their way, justified, good and necessary. Today there is a passion for research, planning and investigation. This application of our intelligence is essential and is of great value for coping with life. When we investigate, plan and arrange our lives, we are always reckoning with the given circumstances. The reckoning mind calculates and has to calculate. It weighs up the more successful possibilities. But because it is always involved with a particular instance, it is not able to engage in reflection. It is not reflective thinking. It is not thinking that ponders on the significance that lies in everything that exists.

What happens when a man becomes reflective? He looks into the distance, into what is unattainable and nevertheless absolutely necessary, or what he cannot control and on what nevertheless his fate as a human being depends. Reflection is a calm, patient and serene kind of thought. It is remarkably simple and quiet. Nor is it difficult or "high". We can reflect about everything. Thus, when we reflect we by no means need any exalted object. It is enough to linger over what is at hand, to consider what is closest to us. It is true that this kind of reflection is not particularly valuable in the discharge of our current business. But it brings order into our life and creates a basis for all our coping with the world.

With this attitude of mind let us now reflect on a virtue that hardly appears in our lists, but without which we could not manage our life. It is called serenity. It makes even the most strenuous exertions simple, it gives an inner balance to a soul that is anchored in God and the world. It is the unreserved opening up of the whole of life, the highest realization of purity in our world; the resolute openness of a trusting heart; openness to the world and openness to God.

It takes a lot of self-control and inner grandeur to remain calm when the tribulations of the world and the inner alienation from God of our own being torment our soul, to preserve discipline and measure when everything is apparently going wrong in our life. It is easy to remain calm when we are blasé, when the situations of life do not take hold of us, when we are not profoundly stirred up by pain and suffering or even by an overwhelming joy. This is easy; but it shows only lack of interest, blunted sensibilities. But what do we do with our own life when we live intensely, when we are wholly exposed to the demands of being, when we experience joy and pain in the innermost fibres of our existence, when we try to be close to all things, events and persons? How do we remain serene at these times?

Here serenity becomes a virtue, an attitude in the world that we have worked hard and suffered to acquire. If we have achieved that attitude that Gertrud von le Fort describes in her poem *An die Freude* ("To Joy"), then we are a person who stands in the world unshakably and is able to offer support and hope. She says in the poem:

> And let the pain burn, pain, I am glad.
> I will call you joy, joy that is darkly clad.

We are attempting here to find a new home in the world that has become so unlike a home. But we shall do this only if we exert ourselves. A home is something that always has to be worked for. A home is an inner event: the quiet security of a soul that is moving towards eternity in the earthly sphere. This kind of home is not tied to a place. It is an attitude, and one that is well described by Martin Heidegger: "Serenity towards things and openness to the mystery belong together. They give us the possibility of living in the world in a wholly different way. They promise us a new ground and foundation on which we can stand and continue to live within the . . . world, not endangered by it." An important text. The philosopher is seeking here a new ground and soil, a new home for modern man. He says that in the modern world these can be acquired only in an inner way. Man must take root in his own being. And this root in his own being is called serenity. Through it, and through it alone, are we able to stand and continue to live in the world. He says that he and his friends will acquire from serenity a "different way of living in the world". What are the conditions of this new way of life and experience?

1. Serenity towards things.—Among "things" Heidegger understands the whole world of experience, men, events, nature, destiny, joy, suffering, pain, happiness and unhappiness. And by serenity he means "nearness". We must become involved (*uns einlassen*) with all this. This is our essential task in the world: To experience our world, to be close to everything that lives and moves in it. We are absolutely "creatures of the earth".

2. In this home of things we must, however, feel ourselves to be homeless.—Only in this way are we able to manage our own existence. Heidegger calls this attitude "openness to the mystery". By this he means an inner openness towards what is wholly other, towards a mystery to which perhaps we cannot give a name (otherwise it would not be a mystery) and which, nevertheless, we experience intensely in all the movements of our existence and in all the situations of our life.

3. Closeness to the creaturely and closeness to the absolute.—From this there grows a new home in the world; an inner home. A quiet being together with all the things of the earth—and a quiet openness to the challenge of an absolute power. It is the equipoise of a being that is plunged into the world (into a world of suffering, joy and death) and at the same time always longs for something that is wholly other, a being that must not lose through its closeness to things his closeness to the absolute—and *vice versa*. It is the attitude of a being who is at peace in the world, who can let all the events of destiny come upon him and still remain in God, firm in the hope of an absolute perfection. "Serenity towards things and openness to the mystery"—this is our new home in a world that has become unhomely. Heraclitus of Ephesus, called the "dark", of whose writings we have today only a few fragments, described the task of the philosopher (of a man who pene-

trates to the being of things) once by the single word
"*anchibasie*". This means "approaching" or drawing near. This
word expresses excellently the nature of serenity, of the virtue
that tries to create a closeness both to the creaturely and to
the absolute. More exactly it means: "to go close" or "to give
oneself to closeness". This means to impart a nearness to
everything. As a miserable creature. To everything: both to
the earth as to God. How can I do this? How can I be serene,
that is, admitted into an existential closeness to the universe?

Here our thinking must leave the philosophical sphere.
Only one man lived in absolute closeness to things and in an
equally absolute closeness to God, and this man was God,
Jesus Christ. That is why he is the only man who can teach
us true closeness, true "approaching". He has spoken to us
words that reveal the innermost truth of things and the innermost truth of the mystery.

Let us look a little more closely at the speaking of Christ.
He speaks a language that has been formed and wholly
clarified in the grave circumstances of human life. Mary
taught the child Jesus this language; perhaps he even took
over his unique emphasis and pronunciation from his mother.
But then, after long silence, came the point when he began to
tear away the veil of the earthly. Through the earthly there
suddenly shone the divine, that which could not be touched.
More and more frequently his words amazed his listeners, as
the Gospel relates. His language became mature, laden with
eternal significance and powerful. He was able to release sick
men, the possessed, the restless and the sinners with the
power of his speech. It is what we long for ourselves, in difficult hours, when we would like to help others. If only we had
the language of essential nearness! If only our language could
undo chains and dispel obscurities! Christ was able to do it.
And then the heaviness of his divine-human fate came upon
him. And this made his language even calmer, even more
surrounded by silence. Right up to the cross. And from the
cross we hear only a few words from his dry and tormented
mouth. These words of the dying god-man shouted out into a
world waiting for salvation show us that there is such a thing

in the world as an absolute nearness. In silence, in the death struggle, in prayer, in the gravest hours of life, there are words of nearness that can be won.

The gospels record seven words from Christ on the cross. If we want to reflect meditatively on the virtue of serenity, then there is no better way than to receive these words of the dying redeemer as far as is possible into our soul: calmly, kindly, and receptively. These seven sentences bring us the unity of the world, closeness to things, and union with God. In it our salvation takes place.

The first word: *"Father, forgive them; for they know not what they do."*

The Evangelist Luke has recorded this word for us (Luke 23. 34). Christ can do nothing more. His hands and his feet are nailed to the cross. He can still speak, painfully, brokenly, but from a soul that seeks closeness. In these words there is total forgiveness, a great love for all being. Christ asks for forgiveness for those who condemned and crucified him. He finds for them a last excuse. He says: We men do not know what we are doing.

We must take this word seriously. We are living in an existential ignorance. Something dull and blunted dominates our thinking. We do not know what is essential and what meaningless, where we come from and where we are going. We sense something great and when it stands before us we do not recognize it. In the last tragedy of his life Christ has the insight that one cannot condemn any man, one must not condemn any man. He does not know what he is doing. Above all those who pretend that they know exactly what they are doing. We are all stumbling in the dark; not necessarily because of evil, but because of a strange dullness of our feeling and experience. We are all still children who do not know their way about the world that contains inestimable mysteries within it. No man can be condemned in his eternal being. What we must say to him is always the word of forgiveness. This is the attitude of ultimate serenity. Always be ready to forgive others in your heart, even against good arguments and proofs. A man who can still find an excuse for others is close to all men. He does not close his eyes, he knows where and when evil happens, he does not judge. He knows how much darkness rules in the human soul, how little we know of the motives for any action, perhaps an evil one. Look for an excuse for others; look desperately if necessary; you will always find something with which you can forgive your neighbour. If you cannot find anything at all, then speak the words of Christ: "They know not what they do."

Thus forgiveness is the first condition of the closeness to the world of men. No man can support the burden of his own guilt who does not forgive others, who does not pardon them from the beginning. This is genuine nearness to men, even into their guilt; the attitude of the radical acceptance of our brokenness; the love of the ignorant and blunted creature—which we all are. Our world needs this attitude. Our world needs this kind of priest in the confessional. Our world needs men such as Christ who can always say at the end, even though they have no proof left: "They know not what they do."

But this essential forgiveness and release from guilt is not humanly possible. Hatred, antipathy, the will to dominate, and resentment must be overcome. That is why there is the radical forgiveness of our being by Christ in prayer. This essential nearness to the creature, in his very inadequacies, can only take place in an openness to the absolute mystery, to God. This is the other side of this mysterious process. Serenity is possible only if man thinks in terms of God. Of a God who cannot deceive anyone, who has himself included sin in his divine plan of salvation, whose Church can sing on Easter night: *"Felix culpa"*—"happy sin".

From this perspective, then, it is not so important what happens to us on earth. Neither in sin nor in virtue have we really known what we were doing. Our true life has not yet appeared here on earth. The important thing, the only significant thing in our life is that we bring more goodness and love into the world. Not that we stand on our right to punish and condemn. What is the good of that? Whom does that make happy? It is time today, we think, to realize that universal sympathy that breaks forth from that painful and broken prayer of Christ: "Father, forgive them, for they know not what they do." In it the infinite goodness of God covers our human frailty. That is why Christ, the God-man, came to us: in order to speak this word. From this attitude of total forgiveness come happiness, peace and quiet understanding. Forgiveness even to those who perhaps want to destroy our life. We are serene in the world. Nothing makes us excited. No man was able to find this path to inner peace, only God, the God-man, and it was the God-man on the cross.

The second word: *"Truly, I say to you, today you will be with me in Paradise."*

It is again the Evangelist Luke, the Evangelist of mercy, who has recorded this second word for us (Luke 23. 43). Here something still deeper breaks forth from the soul of Christ. Not only forgiveness, but also promise. In his broken state he can still give a completely shattered man a last hope. Whether this man understood what he was promised is not of much importance. The main thing was the phrase "with me". That means: "I am with you; you are not abandoned. It does not matter to me what you have done. Perhaps you have done bad things. But for me that is of no importance now. We are now standing both together, we are both nailed to the cross. Let us both forget what has happened. We both still have a hope. Those below who have crucified us do not yet know the nature of this hope. In the best moments of their lives they have a faint sense of it: in their dreams, in their longings, in moments in which they feel happy. But we are unhappy. That is why we know, we two, that this fate cannot be the end. Not because the creature could live forever, but from the mercy of God. And this mercy I promise to you, now, when we are both abandoned to the inescapable. Your life still has a final way out. And this way out is called heaven. There we will finally awake. Everything else was only a prelude, not unimportant, but in a profound sense meaningless. Did you imagine that you could offend God?

He is far too great for that! You have only hurt yourself and your neighbour. You have perhaps only another moment to live. It is good that you now think of all that there has been in your life of beauty, of longing, of hope, gather all that together and then everything is all right. Have hope! Do not let hate rise out of your soul."

Perhaps these brief words of Christ sounded like this in the ear of the thief. They were words of total promise. Here Christ affirmed the essentialness of a being; not the deceptive and transient surface, but his inner longing. The longing for goodness, perfection, selflessness. And to this inner part he promised eternity. With this he has thrown over all the ideas of our human order, indeed of our "morality". He judges a man—fundamentally—according to the hidden longing of his heart, even if this man cannot give to this longing a name. Even if he knows nothing of God. It is enough for him if man has a positive longing in a hidden corner of his soul; perhaps also if he has in himself a longing for this longing. This is the deepest reality of the human soul. The longing is the ultimate criterion.

This longing, the most inward and essential part of our being, will one day unfold towards fulfilment and perfection, into an eternal life. Thomas Aquinas described this state in a beautiful prayer, in the prayer for the grace of contemplation: "Please give, O boundless giver, to my body the beauty of transparency, the capacity of penetration, sensitivity of feeling, and the power of immortality." This is eternal life: everything awakens to brightness and transparency and becomes beautiful and luminous; space and time are overcome; man stands always whither his longing draws him; everything becomes fine and subtle; suffering is banished for ever; only infinite joy lives in us, continuing into infinity. Transparent beauty, the capacity of omnipresence, sensitivity of feeling, power of immortality: this is heaven, our eternal home. And this is promised to us all by a man who is totally honest because he stands at the edge of death, by a suffering man. We should always note what a suffering man says.

It is strange that suffering in our world is the vessel of love.

In suffering we come to a frontier; we must be honest and communicate to others—perhaps haltingly—something of the experiences we have undergone. And the essential communication in suffering is: have hope, life cannot simply be what we experience here; be calm, even in suffering, even in the face of death. No destiny can shatter us, because our life is only something provisional, something unfinished. Our life begins only when we reach heaven. Try to laugh, create joy, radiate goodness into the world: then you will certainly go to heaven. Everything else is unimportant. This is serenity. Peace, the peace won by a soul that can be wounded by so many blows. This essential peace of soul we can acquire only by giving hope to others.

The third word: *"Woman, behold, your son! . . . Behold your mother!"*

Forgiveness and promise—we have still not exhausted the meaning of the word "serenity". Christ gives his mother to the disciple John. He gives everything away. Even what is dearest to him. Giving away is an essential condition of serenity. We come close to men only if we give them something. The most important present is our own presence, our being with them. We must give ourselves, to the very end. Everything that we have. This is perhaps the most difficult thing that love can do: self-giving. To the end. Disappointment, weariness: they are there, they eat away our life. But true love overcomes all that. It sustains life by making it a present of its own self. To behave in this way gives being more hope, future, vitality, expectation, and confidence. If we do not do this, what is the point of our life? But how do we sustain the life of others? How can we give everything away? How can we give to finite being this ultimate nearness?

In living from the mystery. From the mystery that one cannot give away anything that will not return as an infinite gift to us. From the mystery that we lose everything we keep to ourselves and lose nothing that we give away. But we can do this only from God. Everything that we give away remains preserved with God and constitutes our eternal future. We can also live differently. We can keep everything that we have acquired in life. But are we happy? Here a man has even given away his mother, the dearest thing of his life. Now he has nothing left, nothing at all. This is the happiness of the cross: not to have anything left. And yet forgiveness, promise and giving—these were all easy.

The fourth word: "*My God, my God, why hast thou forsaken me?*"

The Lord gives his nearness to all man. And he himself accepts absolute loneliness. He feels himself abandoned by him with whom he is essentially one, so that he can be one with us. He accepts the sadness of man. God takes sides: the side of the lonely and the abandoned, of those who have no more hope. Strange though it may sound, abandonment is a condition of understanding man. All of us are lonely. Often we do not realize how lonely we are, how "God-forsaken". According to this word of Christ the "godless" are not our enemies but our friends. Those who experience what Christ suffered on the cross. No one can say how it was possible that God felt himself abandoned by God. But our own experience confirms that only someone who feels himself totally abandoned can give to men total nearness. Why?

Because precisely in human abandonment—in abandonment that is humanly experienced—we discover that there is an ultimate security; a security that is no longer a part of our human nature. That there is a hope against hope. That God is greater than what we think about him. That God is precisely the one whom we can experience only in what we are not. This is the message of Christ on the cross: it is good to feel lonely and abandoned, to be totally unvisited, unknown and without nearness. If we can overcome this, if we can, in spite of everything, feel the hope that is born of hopelessness, then we have achieved something, then we have overcome the darkness by our own strength. We have faced extreme darkness and danger and precisely at this essential point of the world said "no". In abandonment we find peace, because —precisely in this abandonment—we are able to free others from their loneliness. We can say to them: I have been through it all too and found that God is still nearer. He is so near that we can no longer see him. Have trust, all will be well; not as well as you imagined, but better. This is the serenity that springs from the extreme of human suffering.

The fifth word: *"Jesus . . . said (to fulfil the scripture), 'I thirst'."*

For those present this was the cry of a man whose throat is parched by death, who asks for a little help, some relief. For a few chosen ones this word had a deeper meaning; for those who knew or sensed that this man was God himself. God himself asks us for help. In this he presents us with a new and indescribable nearness. We are able, and admit it, to help God. God asks us for a sip of water. In this he is pointing the way for us also: we should be prepared to accept human goodness. We should receive the gift of goodness and benevolence with humility.

Thus, letting oneself be helped is part of serenity. Pride rejects help and pushes away the hand of mercy. God lets himself be helped. He asks for help. He knows that man can exist only if he is able to help. He does this, as revelation explicitly tells us, "to fulfil the scripture". The "scripture" means here God's plan for mankind, the self-revelation of the absolute and the revelation of the human heart in the face of the absolute. And this total union of the creature with his creator can take place (in its fullness) only if the creature can receive the gift, the help of another creature. If man can find the courage to let himself be helped bodily and spiritually by a friend, by a priest, by a good man. If he does not entrench himself behind his own wretchedness. If he seizes a hand. Help me, I am lost! This desperate cry arouses life in the world, it awakens mercy and goodness. Only a man who relies on the help of his friends can be serene. Now I can sleep in peace. My friends are watching; they are guarding my own life better than I myself. No friend of Christ was able to give him a refreshing drink in his agony. They would have done it so readily. And he would have happily accepted this help.

Perhaps it was better like that. In the longing of wanting to help and not being able to, perhaps the soul of the friends of Christ penetrated still more deeply into the mystery.

It is enough if one wants to help, even if one cannot. It is enough that we have the wish in our soul always to help whenever we can. If it really is not possible, we accompany the man we love with our wishes and our prayers. And we know that in this we are helping him; we are helping him because he accepts our help and makes us capable of helping. We do not give our gifts to him in this moment, but our own being. In this way there comes into being in the world—in a truly human way, though originating in God—a peace, a quiet community in being together, a new dimension in serenity.

The sixth word: "'It is finished': and he bowed his head and gave up his spirit."

The direct meaning of these words was doubtless: I am at the end; I can't go on; I am "finished", emptied, lost. There is nothing left of me. I can do nothing more. My hands and my feet are nailed to the cross. I have done everything that a man was able to do. I have forgiven my torturers; I have given to every man, even to the worst criminal, the last hope; I have given away everything that was dear to me, even my mother; I have accepted every abandonment in order to be near to all men. Now it is enough; I am finished. I cannot do any more. And yet I am enduring. Because I know that there is no end; that you, my God, will soon take me up into the final fulfilment.

God has lived our life right up to its final fulfilment. Men, leave him alone now. He has told us everything that he was able to. Now he is face to face with the Father. Do not disturb him. He is already with the Father. In the absolute mystery. His work is perfected. The world is perfected, our human nature is perfected, even God has perfected himself. He was never nearer to us than in this moment of total withdrawal. Everything great takes place in loneliness, in the nearness of the absolute at the end of a broken life. A man who is near to God is near to all men and to all creatures.

Here Christ has conquered every human wretchedness; but his victory took place in the abyss of death, in a boundless loneliness. He has given everything away, himself, his thoughts, his judgments, even his God. And now he is alone. And he says: Everything is perfected. Who can understand this mystery? The last word from the cross might help us.

The seventh word: *"Then Jesus, crying with a loud voice, said, 'Father, into thy hands I commit my spirit!'"*

What took place here, on this cross and around it? Apparently very little. A criminal has died between two other criminals. A few women have wept. An insignificant man, tortured to death, has spoken a few stumbling words. And yet here there has taken place the most important event of human existence. A man has gathered together in himself everything that we men are, in hours of loneliness, reflection, peace and insight. And he has then broken out of this life into an unattainable remoteness. We shall never see him again in our life. Only in our death. He has passed over. Over to something or someone whom even he himself could describe only in halting words. He is waiting for us. This means he is waiting for us to realize his spirit in the world, to radiate it into the world. He bowed his head: even in the suffering of death he still affirmed everything that we are: men, wretched men, but beings longing for an eternal fulfilment. He is the affirmation of our being. And his spirit is in the hands of God. This means that it is everywhere. Everywhere where human nearness comes into being; where there is forgiveness; where men are given hope; where a man gives himself; where someone feels himself wholly abandoned; where someone trusts in the kindheartedness of friends; where a man supports the loneliness of his fate and finally, where someone dares to give up his whole life in order to achieve something unattainable: in all these places Christ is already present. Christ is there—and the Church is there. Whether all the sacraments, all the prescriptions of canon law, and the testimony in its total fullness are there—what does it matter? Christ is there, and his spirit is there.

We wanted to speak about the virtue of serenity and have spoken about Christ. Perhaps this was better. We have not developed our own ideas, but presented the man who was able to be totally human because he was God.

9. HONESTY

What is honesty? Who is an upright man? Precisely today we must think about this question. How do we stand upright in this life and in this world?

When I was preparing this section I looked up, as usual, Thomas Aquinas. I was looking for the word *sinceritas*, honesty, but could not find a single example of it. At first I was surprised. How could it be possible? Could it be that the greatest teacher of the Church did not have a word to say about this virtue? Then I looked further and found the word *simplicitas*, simplicity. This was the right track. This tiny shift in the meaning of the word leads us deeper into what we mean. We are not talking here merely about an ethical attitude, but about a quality of being. About the clarity, transparency, purity and luminosity of human life.

One day the disciples came to Jesus and wanted to know what the order would be in that essential sphere of humanity that he called the kingdom. Jesus took a child by the hand, placed it in their midst and said: "Truly, I say to you, whoever does not receive the kingdom of God like a child shall not enter it." In this he set up a criterion. In order to enter into the essentialness of being we must become like children. What does Christ mean when he places this importance on the attitude of a child? Assuredly not something weak or immature. Not a wrong kind of dependence. These words of Christ about the child have often been misused. They have been distorted by sentimental, foolish and inferior thinking. The attitude that Christ calls for here as the criterion of ultimate human authenticity reaches to the very roots of our being. It is "simplicity of heart". In what does it consist?

The idea of its own self does not yet exist in the consciousness of a child; or at least not primarily. The basic movement of its life moves away from itself. It is open. In its consciousness there are things, events and men—and not primarily its own ego. The attitude, then, for which the child is a symbol, is a fundamental innocence of purpose. It is a creative youthfulness, that keeps itself open, that looks, and when it meets something or someone, goes towards it; the capacity to look at what is open, to feel the essential thing and receive it without any intentions towards it; innocence of intention.

According to the words of Christ, therefore, we are to overcome our adulthood, inasmuch as it means acting a part, wilfulness, an artificial relationship to the world, and only external correctness. This becoming young is an inner process. It is a conversion of one's whole being. As a Christian I involve myself in everything, without reserve. The essential thing is taken fully as reality and loved, if I do not hold on to myself or to anything in myself, if I do not look back at myself but let myself go. Children play sometimes in this way, in the simplicity of their hearts. And this is the way that a Christian ought to live.

The phrase "simplicity of heart" arouses today dislike and resistance. That is why it should be spoken. In early Christianity this simplicity was practically the mark of the Christian man. It is a virtue that is not only praised in the Gospel, but stands at its centre. The virtue without which one cannot enter into the kingdom, into nearness to Christ.

Heaven springs from the hearts of the simple. This is a principle of Christian eschatology. In early Christian piety "simplicity of heart" meant the unconditional loyalty of man towards God, the total giving of himself by man to God. A condition of life in which the heart and soul of a man were wholly present in everything that he did. A man with a whole heart: whole in devotion, whole in honesty, whole in friendship, whole in love. This heart is not divided, it is not split. It is not dominated by double goals.

Is this simple, luminous, glowing attitude difficult in the world? Is sincerity difficult? I would say yes. But God says no. How do we become so simple that the truth and fullness of life shine through us? How do we become the sort of man who, as Thomas Aquinas says: "does not say anything but what he really has in his mind"? How do we become men who do not play a double role? Men without that split in our lives that falsifies the whole life of a man? How do we manage without playing a part? We have returned to the question: How do I become a man who is authentic and unified within himself? It says in the Old Testament: "It is not in heaven . . . neither is it beyond the sea . . . but . . . it is . . . in your heart, so that you can do it" (Deut. 30. 12–14).

What does this mean? It means that authenticity is attainable for all men. Even if one has no idea of heaven, even if one has not seen the breadth of the world. Authenticity is an attitude of the heart. We may say that every man is already a Christian, by virtue of being a man. Sincerely lived and honestly experienced humanity contains the possibility of a positive attitude to Christ, even if such a man does not know explicitly about Christ. Every man, whether baptized or not, a "militant atheist" or an "ordinary, automatic atheist", can be confronted with the Christian. Thus, for example, the silent honesty of everyday life can be the form in which many a so-called pagan accepts the unknown God. Someone who has no access to the sacraments and to the revelations of God in his word and yet accepts and performs what is given him to do as a human being and demands realization by him is already an anonymous Christian and has a share in the salvation that Christ brought. Apostolic activity would then be an attempt to bring the Christianity that is already potentially present and realized anonymously in every man to its full and conscious expansion. Wherever man lives honestly as man and as himself, where he experiences longing, discontent and inadequacy, the joy of love or friendship, wherever he is faced with a mortal incomprehensibility, he already comprehends the incomprehensible and places himself in the grace of Christ, even if he is not objectively aware of it and even if he regards himself as an atheist. He has a *votum implicitum* of Church membership. He is a Christian.

A man who has accepted his humanity honestly has accepted the son of man. Ultimately man is explained in terms of the self-emptying of God. This is potentially a fundamentally christological understanding of man. God is present in every sincere movement of the human heart.

But how? This is a question that will cause much difficulty to theologians of the next decades. On the one hand, we must hold firm to the fact that every man can be a Christian, by being an honest man. On the other hand, we ask ourselves: why are we Christians, then? Why do we belong to the Church? The answer is, we think, simple: because we are chosen. Not chosen for salvation. Every man can achieve this. But we are chosen to bear witness, to be transparent to the absolute. We have the task of concentrating within ourselves the presence of God. We are, as Hans Urs von Balthasar said, the "Ernstfall".[7] It is for us to make visible the fact that the spirit of Christ is present, not just anonymously, but explicitly.

Let us take up an idea of Mario von Galli: The Holy Spirit came down on everyone gathered in the room of the Last Supper. The people there, as Scripture clearly states, were women, the relatives of Jesus, and Joseph the Just. They were all speaking as the spirit inspired them. To every Christian today also confirmation is given as a sacrament so that, under the guidance of the Holy Spirit, he can make his testimony for Christ. No one is excluded from this. All have to realize this transparency to God in their lives, which is what makes them witnesses of God in the world. Thus transparency to God, what shines through, the simple, the unambiguous is the real task of Christians in the world. This is a charismatic action.

A charism is an influence of the Holy Spirit on the individual believer, a man can never force it, the official organs of the Church cannot predict it, and it is not even given by the sacraments. And yet it is part of the nature of the Church, it is possible everywhere, but must always be newly discovered and accepted. It is always a new impulse of the spirit of God, who confronts the Church with its new presence.

Ignatius of Loyola says in the fifteenth note of his *Exercises* that the master of the exercises should "let the creator speak

[7] Lit. the "serious case", that is, in this context, those aware of their critical existential situation.—Trans.

directly to his creature and the creature with his creator". Here he formulated the basic law of the working of individual grace in the Church. And if there are these direct influences of the Holy Spirit in the life of each one of us, then the individual has the Christian duty and task to recognize these influences in his own life. But he must be prepared for them. The official Church cannot and must not take from the individual the burden of his task. And the individual Christian does not have the right to entrench himself behind official Church directives.

But are Christians prepared to recognize God's direct inspirations in their individual lives? Personal spiritual direction, listening to the voice of the Holy Spirit and the distinguishing of spirits are by no means esoteric and exclusive disciplines, but forms of everyday Christian living. It is not enough to be a devout, proper and obedient Christian if we want to fulfil our individual Christian testimony. The Holy Spirit has reserved to itself the revelation of this destiny. Spiritual direction can merely try to develop in individual Christians that openness of the heart that observes the coming of the Spirit and readily accepts it.

As a Christian I have the task of doing more; that individual and irreplaceable thing that makes my life transparent, that transforms it into a transparency of God. We must be witnesses by being Christians. We must become for our fellow men a direct grace, which is irreplaceable because it is charismatically individual, we must be a present of God to our friends. The kingdom of God must be "built up" in us in grace. This is perhaps the profoundest significance of that virtue which the German language describes as *Aufrichtigkeit*. How do we achieve it? What is the inner structure of this charismatic quality of "being lifted up straight"?

In the Second Letter to the Corinthians (6. 2–10) the apostle Paul describes the true witness of the absolute in the world in the following way:

Now is the acceptable time; behold, now is the day of salvation. We put no obstacle in any one's way, so that no fault may be found with our ministry, but as servants of God we commend ourselves in every way: through great endurance, in afflictions, hardships, calamities, beatings, imprisonments, tumults, labours, watching, hunger; by purity, knowledge, forbearance, kindness, the Holy Spirit, genuine love, truthful speech, and the power of God; with the weapons of righteousness for the right hand and for the left; in honour and dishonour, in ill repute and good repute. We are treated as impostors, and yet are true; as unknown, and yet as well known; as dying, and behold we live; as punished, and yet not killed; as sorrowful, yet always rejoicing; as poor, yet making many rich; as having nothing, and yet possessing everything.

The heart of this dialectically constructed passage of Scripture is the list of the four qualities of charismatic honesty: purity, knowledge, forbearance, and kindness. Let us comment on them briefly.

Purity

In the Greek text this is the hard, almost intranslatable word "*hagnótes*". This is something dazzling, that power that stirs our heart. It is a Christian duty to realize this. Those realities that are directly in contact with the absolute are called in Scripture "*hagnoi*". Through them God works directly, as in the sacraments, pouring in, touching and laying hold of us. They are places of showing, of open confessing and of honest being. Light becomes being in them. This quality of luminously standing upright is seen in Scripture in the figure of the deacon Stephen, a man of tremendous spiritual power. We know from the seventh chapter of Acts how Stephen was brought to court and accused. He speaks about God's plan of salvation. Everyone feels the power of his words. We read that "gazing at him, all who sat in the council saw that his face was like the face of an angel". And then a paroxysm of hate gathered against this man filled with the light of God. All become of one mind in hate. They hurl stones at him until this intolerable light on his face fades away. It is an intensely impressive event. It shows the influence of this light of God in a man, the influence of honesty. A man filled with the dazzling light of divinity stands there; he makes the others tremble; his being is determined by a strange, incomprehensible and shattering power; he is filled with forces that are foreign to other men. This shattering quality comes from his devotion to God. To shine becomes for him the act of being: he has become inwardly luminous. A mighty sacrifice of life is taking place here, something that is psychologically inexplicable. A flame is burning. Piece by piece this man throws his life into this flame. But everything is contained in his sacrifice; the whole of Christian existence; the whole of human life. This man stands upright. He is an upright man. He knows that here, where he has to sacrifice himself, there is fulfilment; a life that is luminous and burning, and bearing witness by its honest integrity to the holiness of the absolute. And to such a life we are all called—in the "moment of crisis", but also in everyday life.

Knowledge

The Greek word here is "*gnōsis*". This is not knowledge that leads to academic degrees. Here the inner vision of things is meant. Familiarity with the whole of life and with the absolute. A knowledge that can come only from prayer. It is a knowledge that is held by love. That knowledge in which man comprehends more and more in faith the incomprehensible love of God, and lets himself be laid hold of by this love as the ultimate authentic thing. A knowledge of one's own eternal destiny. A knowledge that of its nature is directed towards contemplation, towards the calm dwelling of man in the presence of the utterly mysterious and unnamable, in the presence of what we describe by the word "God". It is not only knowledge, it is wisdom. How few truly wise men there are today, and how badly we need them! Wisdom knows reality in terms of God and in its relations back to him. It interprets the specific knowledge of God. Christian knowledge in this sense is born when we are seized by the love of God.

This knowledge of God, however, does not come essentially through our reason. It is the result of living action. Through patient, active and living practice we achieve a "connaturality", an "existential relationship" with God. Man becomes familiar with the absolute, with its absolute mystery. He experiences the presence of the infinite in finite reality. He sees God in all things. In all the actions and decisions of his life there is always contained a feeling of the absolute—however deep down, weak and changing. This knowledge of the divine penetrates gradually all our other knowledge. It becomes our destiny. Longing springs up in our heart; we listen to the voice of God; we call him and are ready for him. This is the "knowledge that surpasses all knowledge", of which Scripture speaks. Only this kind of knowledge makes us true witnesses and raises us up. We become Christians, who have stepped into a loving and knowing central relationship with Christ, men whom to be near is to be near God.

Forbearance[8]

Forbearance is more than patience. It is a particular kind of "slowness": slowness to anger, the length of time one needs in order to become angry. In the book *Exodus* we read of God that he is a merciful and compassionate God, slow to anger and rich in goodness and faithfulness. The echo of this primal revelation goes through the whole Old Testament. For God to be forbearing means even that he suffers insults without punishing them. Thus a man who is slow to anger, slow to be discouraged, a man who can wait and endure is a special witness of God, he realizes that transparency to the absolute that we have called honesty.

Forbearance is a quality of selfless love. It is the opposite of

[8] "Langmut", lit. "slow-mindedness".—Trans.

indifference. It is the conquest of one's own heart that has become kindly towards others. It consists in not avenging wrong, in not seeking revenge, of renouncing punishment, of restraining the feeling of anger and resentment in the heart, indeed of not even feeling it.

The man who has overcome inwardly his despair of man and changed it into compassion has performed one of the greatest acts of charismatic love, of testifying to God, of Christian honesty: this is raised-up being that bears witness. In such a life it can appear that the wholly other, that which can no longer be explained in human terms, that God, truly exists and has power over human hearts. To do this not only when our inner *élan* urges us to it, but constantly, even in a state of tiredness and exhaustion, when one is fed up, even when a feeling of revulsion gathers at the bottom of our soul, when offences discolour our own being, when our heart is weary, this is Christian testimony.

Kindness

Kindness is expressed by Paul in a word that he likes using for God himself. We could translate the Greek word "*chrestótes*" by friendliness and thus emphasize the mild and gentle side of the quality. There is a triumphant power of grace, a beauty of being that comes from God. Being becomes "powerful with love" and precisely thus the testimony of an absolute love. As witnesses of Christ we have the task of being so kind that something shines in us of what the apostles experienced in Christ: "The love of God towards men lit up his face." It is one of the most important tasks of Christians to bear testimony to this essential characteristic of Christ. Inner grandeur, that is, being sensitive to the other being, is an essential element of the charismatic testimony. Through this the Christian becomes fully the gift of God to his fellow men and raises up the figure of Christ in the world. In this there is a judgment of one's own self and also a judgment of the world. Judgment takes place through kindness.

Honesty as judgment

It must be possible for man to give away everything. His whole life must pass through a test. We live still in a strangely confused world. We do not know the point of our life and what will become of us. We do not yet experience the authentic. Could we, just as we are, enter heaven? A heaven that means total transparency of being?

This is why man must pass through a fire, through purgatory. Fire is here an image. The image of purging, of purification, of passing into a state in which everything becomes open, openly visible and transparent to the very bottom of our being. Could we bear this? Could we live in such a world, live happily? No! We would be destroyed by this transparency of our being. Would not heaven then be for us "hell"?

But if God were to give us the opportunity of meeting him, of standing before him in total honesty, then every man would be able to and have to recognize that God is there, the God of absolute and unswerving friendship. What would man say then? To this God? I think he would say: "I am nothing, I am truly nothing. I cannot receive what your love expects of me, what you want to give me. I have become utterly and finally humble." This is the essence of purgatory.

But nothing is denied us after we have renounced. In purgatory everything can be saved and comforted, to the very depth of the cosmos. Man has finally a chance of giving away everything that he is. It will be a miracle of light, dark forms will become friendly and rigid ones be loosed, mysterious and confused ones will become simple and clear. Man will become the present of God to the universe, to the heart of his fellow men. Life will become glowing. There humanity will be raised up and become honest.[9] The hard proliferating layers of dishonesty, the layers of selfishness, of egoism, will be borne away. True human life will open itself. We are not yet really living. Our life is a beginning. It is a movement of

[9] "aufgerichtet" and "aufrichtig".

growth towards heaven. The universe evolves out of an original state of being towards life. Life perfects itself by changing within us men to spirit. Spirit takes it over, when it recognizes God and gives itself to him in love. The union with God then brings the whole universe into eternal fulfilment. This is attainable for us men, namely, through the fire of the encounter with God. God creates the world by giving it the power to work its way and raise itself up to him in a process that lasts billions of years. The end is the real beginning, the beginning of absolute honesty. On the one hand, it says: "What no eye has seen, no ear has heard, what has been known in the heart of no man, God has prepared for those who love him." Thus heaven is still a long way off. It is something that does not yet exist. It is radically different. But on the other hand, heaven is already near to us, with the resurrection and ascension of Christ it has already begun. The forces of the world to come have already laid hold on us.

Christianity regards the resurrection of Christ not as the private fate of our Lord, but at the same time the first sign of the fact that in our world everything has become different, in the real and decisive depth of reality. The Easter event is not a limited and separate phenomenon, but the sacred destiny of the whole world. In his resurrection Christ spoke over the whole universe his word, his word that creates reality: It has begun: "Behold, I make all things new". Heaven, then, is still a long way from us. But it is also near to us, absolutely related to us. The Christian lives in this tension as a Christian. He is somehow already in heaven, but in a heaven that still has to come. Heaven appears to us in undramatic forms, in reflections.

Heaven is a condition of human authenticity. The accent is on both words. Heaven is human. The Lord promised to everyone his own personal happiness in heaven. That for which he most longs. Water to the Samaritan, the bread of life to the people of Capharnaum, full nets to the fishermen, great herds and evergreen pastures to the shepherds, and precious pearls to the merchants. And to us all, always an eternal banquet, a wedding: a symbol of infinite happiness in the possession of that person who is dearest to us in life. The apostles then promised the Greeks what brought them most happiness: knowledge, wisdom, security, transparent being, built up out of shining precious stones. Heaven, then, is being that is lived intensely and wholly, with honesty and sincerity. Not a realm of ideas, but the infinitely increased perfection of human life, of our sense perceptions, which "grasp" in heaven God as a gift. In heaven that inexpressible thing will take place for which the Church prays: "*Accende lumen sensibus*." The light of God will shine out before all our senses. There will take place what the mystics and all deeply religious people have already experienced in various images: God will be heard, touched, and tasted by us.

Thus in heaven all things of the spirit will be transformed into the sphere of the senses, and all things of the senses into the sphere of the spirit. Even God. And man becomes aware of the whole of reality, of the saved world. This ultimate perfection, heaven, is the final nearness of God, the sharing in God. True, his infinite plenitude cannot be exhausted by any creature. Our being cannot coincide wholly with God's inexhaustible being. Thus every fulfilment is at the same time the beginning of a greater fulfilment. Thus heaven is essentially a boundless dynamic. Everything static passes in heaven into an infinite dynamic that continues into eternity. Perfection is eternal change. God judges no one. He does not need to. He reveals his love. And in death, man judges himself finally in relation to this love. If he says yes to this love, even if it is at the last moment, at the moment of his death, everything is all right. God lovingly receives his creature, where and when it comes towards him. Could we not reinterpret the various historical pericopes of Scripture in the light of that passage in John, which says: "For God so loved the world that he gave his only Son, that whoever believes in him should not perish but have eternal life. For God sent the Son into the world, not to condemn the world, but that the world might be saved through him. He who believes in him is not condemned; he who does not believe is condemned already" (3. 16–18)?

Accordingly, judgment is basically self-judgment. God will say to us in the judgment: "You have done many bad things. Never mind. I have forgotten everything. Come to me. What you have done is done. It is not so important. Just come to me. I shall receive you. Just as you are. In all your wretchedness." Is not this the true greatness of God? Is not this a testimony for what Scripture says of him that God is greater than our heart? He is far too great a Lord. Only we can condemn ourselves. Judged, raised-up being[10] comes from our own decision.

No one is damned, just because fate, because chance willed it. Can eternal self-damnation depend on chance? Every man must have the possibility of at least once, even in death, meeting our Lord, Jesus Christ. To know him absolutely personally.

What, then, do purgatory and judgment mean? They mean first of all that we are not yet standing "properly"[11] in our life, that we cannot yet move into the sphere of authenticity. But also that it is possible for us to move into it. Our being is broken, that is true. It must be raised up, into heaven, into a perfection that never ends. Purgatory and judgment, then, are not mythical, mythological events, but what we daily experience in our lives: the urge and longing for truth, that is, for honest integrity. We must one day make order in our lives, radically.

The achievement of this conversion, this change, this turning, is the centre of Christian living. Here we are offered a criterion. It is a far more important criterion than martyrdom. It is the criterion, the essential mark of the cross. Total self-surrender, in which our own being becomes transparent, letting the absolute shine through. In its heart it is humility.

10 "gerichtet", "aufrichtig".
11 "richtig".

10. HUMILITY

The centre of human life, of a life that is lived honestly, is humility, self-limitation. But self-limitation is already an implicit acknowledgement of God. It is the capacity, the virtue that has been acquired perhaps with difficulty, of not placing oneself in the centre of events and interest. Let us take up here a fine thought of Cardinal Journet: In a true sense, but one that is hard to define, humility is already adoration. Life is not long enough to speak about humility and to praise it as it should be praised. And no life is long enough to realize humility fully, that is, to pass wholly into the simplicity of being. For humility is the full recognition of an absolute boundary.

Thus, to speak about humility means basically to speak about God. What does it mean: To support God, to acknowledge him in such a way that one's own life shrinks before him, but in precisely this becomes great? It requires a spiritual greatness to accept greatness, to limit oneself in the face of the great. How do we become so great that we can be humble?

Humility is an experience of the absolute, the experience of an absolute boundary and of absolute greatness beyond it. The attitude of humility is justified and livable only if an absolute exists, the absolute God. Humility is not "lowness". It is anchored in the same depth of the soul as magnanimity and generosity. It is by no means self-contempt. Quite the contrary: it is respect for the infinite that dwells within us, but with which we are not identical. In order to be humble we must live in the presence of the absolute; in friendship and in love. We all live, consciously or unconsciously, in the presence of God. But this presence takes place within a broken existence. Humility, therefore, would be simply to endure this tension of being exposed to God and of being broken oneself.

But who is this God to whom we are exposed? What is his

face like? Here is a God, whom we experience everywhere, in all the motions of our heart, but yet is not part of the structure of our world. How does a man live who has experienced God? How does he live his life in the presence of this absolute power that is near to him everywhere and at the same time always absent? How can a man support what the presence of God means? Here I can do nothing but say in Christian honesty the way in which I have experienced God, that is, describe the form of "my God". If we have once described God's being and his presence in the world, then we can say in a few words what human humility is. There are, in particular, five basic tensions between God and man, from which humility grows.

God is light and darkness together

The apostle John said of God: "God is light; in him there is no darkness." But the prophet Isaiah says of God: "You are indeed a hidden God; God, the saviour of Israel." Which of the two is right?

Let us endeavour to approach this paradox of revelation. Is God light? Is he darkness? There are two kinds of darkness. There is a darkness that comes from an excess of light, and there is a darkness that means simply blackness. Too much light or too little, both create darkness. We can even be completely dazzled by light so that we no longer see anything. The purity of being reveals itself to us and it blinds us. It is too near, we cannot see it. God's being is too intense for us, too overwhelming. Here begins the paradox of the clearness of God, the mystery of his closeness to us. His dazzling closeness creates a darkness for us. Today above all, this darkness fills the world. Man seeks something to hold on to. He seeks things; things that he can touch, that he can feel. He seeks a programme of life, a way of coping with existence. But God cannot be found in this way. God is hidden for us precisely through his closeness to us. He is hidden in his light. We can walk beside him like the Emmaus disciples without noticing him. This is bright darkness. He is too bright for our eyes to notice him. There is always a veil, a curtain before his being.

That is why man can never find peace in the world. He sees things, he experiences the world, friendship, love, the happiness of life, and always seeks something behind them, something hidden. We cannot live without God. Nor can we live with him. He is too bright, and, at the same time, too dark. Man speaks so easily and so much of God. If they spoke less of him it would be perhaps easier. The night of God in the world! But yet, a bright night, a blessed night. We are constantly hindered by our own inner blindness from looking into the light of God. Why does God permit all this? Why is his being so dazzling? The question remains: Who is this God before whom we must limit ourselves in order to be human at all? To whom we are exposed in such humiliation? He is a God of darkness and of light.

God is both silence and word

Silence is one of the most impressive events of our life. St Dominic once visited St Francis of Assisi. They embraced each other, and the whole time they said nothing to each other. Not a word. They parted without having said a word. A deeply moving event. God also gives himself to us in silence and through silence. But it is difficult to support this silence of God in our life. We are frightened of it.

The most beautiful words of a man are born in silence. It is, as it were, the glowing furnace of the word, where the most important words, feelings and thoughts are forged. Creative movement begins in silence, in a long quietness. When music becomes very beautiful, it stops. We sense at such moments a mystery. We want to protect this mystery and not mingle it with the things of the world. That is why one is silent.

The extraordinary thing is, however, that the absolute mystery, God, speaks to us nevertheless. But how? This silent God speaks to us in the prophet Hosea: "I will lead you into the wilderness and there I will speak to you." The men to whom God speaks and through whom God speaks to us are always those men whom God led into the wilderness, into the loneliness of suffering, of inner hunger, into unstillable longing, and who became quite still in it. In this kind of silence, full of suffering and longing, those essential words are born of which we have just spoken. Words that are dug out, as it were, with bleeding hands from the depth of the mystery. Once we have heard these words, we can never forget them. Like the words of the Beatitudes. We can understand them quite clearly at once and take them into ourselves, although we never fully understand them. They are too deep for us, and yet we understand them. We understand, for example, what the words of Christ mean when he says that the lowly and the humble are blessed, those who are truly happy. Words about the essence of being are always an inner event, an event of love. "My sheep know my voice", said Christ and meant the humble.

Jesus was the word of God. And yet, or for that very reason: what silence reigned in his soul! He was lonely among us, lonely with that mystery that he called the "Father". The disciples were a long way from understanding. They were always asking him for explanations, especially when he spoke most clearly. He did not become irritable, nor did he rebuff them. There was a great inner peace behind everything. The Evangelist Luke says: "In these days he went out into the hills to pray; and all night he continued in prayer to God. And when it was day, he called his disciples" (6. 12–13).

The silence of Christ, the silence of God! What did God say to his Son when he called to him on the cross? When Joan of Arc was executed in the market place of Rouen she cried out: "Jesus, Jesus!" This desperate cry was heard throughout the whole town, it was so loud, so superhuman, and desperate. But the only answer was the silence of God. Holy humility is living with such a God.

God is the peace that makes us restless

Often we read in the Gospel that when Christ entered a house he said: "Peace be with you." Or: "It is I, fear not." When a priest enters a house, for example, when he brings communion to the sick, the Church requires him to say:

"Peace be to this house and to all who dwell in it." The word "peace", or, more exactly, the obligation to say: "Peace be with you", that is, to speak like this to a person or to friends is an essential word, a key-word of our Christian life and our proclamation. Peace, peacefulness, is the most powerful force in the world. We usually have no idea of how tremendously powerful benevolence and love can be. The peace of God that is to dwell in us can, however, be a heavy responsibility. "God in the heights, you are terrible", almost intolerable, because this intensity of love and friendship commits us to something that we, humanly speaking, can hardly bear.

God asks goodness of us and in doing this commits us to the cross. Since the crucifixion of Christ we know what it means to be wholly good and benevolent in this confusing world; what happens to a man who wants to bring peace and the love of man into the world. But if even the merest shadow falls on us from the radiance of divine peace, then we see things in a quite different light. We see what we have to do in the world. And this affects our attitude to reality, it changes our relationships to men, it changes the tone of our voice, the way we see, even the expression of our face, it may even change it into a smile.

One event of Christ's life shows well this peace. Christ is asleep in the little boat while the storm rages. He is obviously tired. But his heart is awake. The apostles have seen this quiet and peaceful face. It is true that in sleep the face is generally peaceful. But what peace must this face of the incarnate God have radiated! The storm did not waken him, it was not able to. He wanted to sleep and he slept. What he did, he did entirely as a fully integrated man. Even in sleep. None of his actions was inwardly disturbed, only half willed. With him everything happened quietly and automatically. But the anxious voices of his friends did wake him. It was they who were able to wake him. The philosopher Bergson once said: "The voice of a mother, the quietest voice of a mother sounds like thunder to a child that is loved and loves." The apostles woke Christ. But they also disturbed him inwardly (cf. Matt. 8. 23–27).

This is the other side of the mysterious peace of Christ: what unrest, what care the God-man, this quiet God had to bear; he, of all people, who wanted to bring only peace. On the one hand, he was unshakably calm within, because he saw God and was directly united with him. He was carried by the unplumbable peace of eternal being. Blaise Pascal said, however, "The heart of man is an abyss of uncertainty and unrest." What uncertainty and unrest did the incarnate God feel in his heart! Such a patience that once he had to say: "I came to cast fire upon the earth; and would that it were already kindled!"

The emotion of the Redeemer when he stood before the grave of his friend Lazarus is described in the Gospel in the following way: "He was deeply moved in spirit and troubled." This means that he did not restrain by force the movements of his heart. He was able to weep. And it even says in the Gospel: "Jesus wept." He really did weep, not just symbolically, with all the suffering that is contained in weeping. Some words of Christ that are recorded in the synoptic gospels intensify what is suggested here to a degree that is beyond our understanding: "My soul is very sorrowful, even to death." Where does this sadness come from in an infinitely peaceful soul? What does this uncertainty of a totally calm existence mean? The confusion of a soul that sees God? A life that is bathed in the peace of God? It is not really an unrest at all, but distress felt for men. It increases to an agony, in which he begs his Father not to let justice reign, but only love. In this agony there comes an angel to comfort him. What does this mean? A creature comforts God! God has taken human unrest so intensely upon himself that he must be comforted by a finite creature.

We must realize in our own life this peace of God which reveals itself in unrest and care. This is our task, to be performed in grace. If God is love—and that is the definition of his being—then this love must reveal itself as care. Care shows that we love. A mother is anxious if her child is sick or is in difficulties. The unrest of the heart is an expression of true love, which understands the dangers that threaten the loved person. If a mother did not feel anxious, she would not love. We try to project all the love that we experience in our broken lives into God, into absolute love, into *the* love, into boundless love.

If absolute love consists of rest and unrest, then we know what our finite love is like. Christ has gathered the whole unrest of love in his heart. And he endured this. Because he wanted to bring peace, he had to live in unrest. He had to take on himself all the sufferings and tribulations of men, of all men. We do not know how he endured it. He was God. He could endure it.

The great question of our Christian life, however, is: how do we endure it? To deal with this kind of God requires a high degree of humility. The peace of God that changes from love into unrest! This burden of love presses on us also. Sometimes our life seems smashed, and insupportable. But it is good to be crushed by the weight of love. To accept the care of others in love and patience, to be one with them in sufferings and trials, and persist in it: this is humility.

God is the purity that touches us impure men

This is perhaps the most amazing mystery of God. What is purity? It is the existential attitude of a man who says to himself: I want to construct something in the world, something that is beautiful, pure and good, consisting of pure being. This is what God wanted, this was his plan when he created us. This attitude of being he created as a paradise: a direct nearness to everything that is beautiful and good.

Man somehow threw away this chance he was offered. The accounts of the Bible are unclear here. But it is now necessary to build up in ourselves again this transparent, pure and unadulterated being. To be pure means to have an innocence of intention when we think, feel, will and love; to enter into all the questions, all the sufferings, all the brokenness that we encounter; to enter into earthly life, honestly, i.e. not with double goals. If such a man in the simplicity of his heart accepts the burden of kind nearness to life, then he experiences things as they really are. According to Thomas Aquinas purity is basically "*firmitas*": constancy of decision, persisting in love within a world that consists largely of suffering and tribulation. Our goodness is to be revealed to all men.

If a wholly good man were to appear among us we could not support him. His fate would be the cross. That was also the fate of Christ. God has raised the world from nothing, he has made it pure and transparent being. From nothing. This being, this world, constantly falls, at every moment, back into nothingness. Above all within us. That is why we need men who raise up this being again, into what is light, good, friendly and lovable: in short, into being. Otherwise we can give up this world. Nothing will become of it. But God has constantly called men who have grasped in their hearts that this is precisely their task and their fate: to expect nothing but to give everything away.

There are such men; men who have retreated from the world, who have decided in a moment of pure courage to sacrifice themselves entirely to the good. Who want to be nothing but mercy, who just want to be there for God's call and commission. A St Bernard, for example, who withdrew inwardly from the world and wanted nothing other than to stand pure before God. This pure intention of living for God has done an infinite amount of good, perhaps more than parties and movements. Without the humble "yes" of Mary, who was without sin, the incarnation would not have been possible. God wanted to become man; but he could not have become man if our earth had not received him. In the grace of God our earth was able to be concentrated in pure receptivity: in Mary. Doing this makes her for us eternally worthy of reverence and bestows greatness on all the women of the world.

Then Christ appeared among us: honesty, goodness and simplicity. He was there for others. This was what led to his death. Precisely this attitude of mind. He went to sinners, to men who did not have this attitude of mind. As he says constantly in the Gospel, he came to us in order to give to those men the closeness of God.

The despised Zacchaeus, a social outcast, once climbed up a tree to see Christ. When Christ came by he stopped in front of the tree on which little Zacchaeus was sitting. He called up, perhaps smiling to himself: "Zacchaeus, make haste and come down; for I must stay at your house today." He went into the house of the man who was not respected, even despised by others; he was small in stature and had a disreputable profession. This was the man he chose to go to. He lived with him (cf. Luke 19. 1–10). Purity dwells with impurity.

On another occasion there was a woman who had been seduced by her misguided love to become an adulteress. Others wanted to judge her. She was taken before Christ. A poor lost creature. What happened? Christ did not look at the sinner, but her judges; he looked deep into their souls and then said slowly and powerfully: "Let him who is without sin among you cast the first stone." Then he knelt down and started writing in the sand. What he wrote is not recorded in the Gospel. But we are told that all the accusers went away. Purity that touches us impure men. Then we read that the Lord raised his eyes and looked at the woman. All had gone away. He asked her: Has no one condemned you?—A profoundly moving moment. Christ knew well what sin is. But he was too generous to condemn this poor creature and reproach her. He said to her quite simply: "Neither do I condemn you." But he added, precisely because his mission was to bring purity into the world: "Do not sin again" (cf. John 8. 1–11).

How is our life? We contain within ourselves so much darkness and conflict, both conscious and unconscious. How can we experience this merciful God in our condition? There is so much antipathy, dislike, even hate in us—perhaps not in the crudest forms, but in little moments of irritation and touchiness. A thoughtless clumsy word, a clumsy action that was perhaps even well-meant can hurt a man for years afterwards. How can God redeem us, raise us out of this condition? Perhaps only through death, through the total encounter with his purity. In death we will then become very gentle and good. We will say there with our whole being: Lord, I am not worthy.

How does man then dare to approach Christ in this earthly life? How does one dare to go to communion?—God has commanded us to come to him. Just as we are. Our fallenness should not hinder us. But a man must say humbly: Lord, I am not worthy. Like a beggar. A man who really speaks these words and really thinks like this of himself can never communicate unworthily. Only he receives Christ "unworthily" who is proud; who says: Lord, I am worthy.

God is both riches and poverty

He is the wealth that begs from us. Giving is a sign of love. But we can give God nothing. Everything belongs to him. And yet he has created us so that we can give him something. Like parents who give children money so that the children can buy presents for them. The parents then seem surprised and happy. And they are. The child has really given them something. This is love: we give and we receive. We give so that others may have the pleasure of giving back.

With God it is just the same. In his eternal being God depends on no one. In him being is present in absolute plenitude. He is perfect, just as he is, independently of us. Why, then, has God created the world? Because he needs love. How is this possible? This is a mystery. It is a fact that he has created the world out of pure love, for he can do nothing but what is love. The world has been created from an ultimate ground—from love—from a ground that is not grounded in any other ground. Thomas Aquinas calls this love "self-giving". A man also who is truly good must give himself, out of an inner compulsion.

Is it our task to put questions to God? To ask: Why have you placed us within all these difficulties of the world? Why is there all this suffering about us, all the distress and the insecurity? It is true, these are our most troubling questions.

But we shall not be able to answer them if we do not have first the courage to say: I thank you, my God, for creating me as I am. In moments of despair it is very difficult to say these words. And yet, even in such moments, we must be able to say as Christians—and this is "heroic" humility—I thank you, God, that you have created me. You have called me into being in order to create out of this world by friendship and goodness something new. It is my task to raise the world higher and help my friends. Everything else will be solved of itself.

But this is not the whole truth. We are loved still more by God. God has created us to make a response. Christ has visited us, he has sought us. He has knocked on our door. He suffered terrible weariness in doing this. There is a poem in the Church's mass for the dead, the sequence *"Dies irae, dies illa"*. It contains a very beautiful verse that one might translate in the following way: "When you sought me, you became so tired that you had to sit down. On the cross you have redeemed me in your suffering. Such suffering must not be in vain."

In the same way Jesus also sat by Jacob's well, in the burning heat of noonday. He was very tired. He went there in order to meet someone. A sinner. If one follows the journeys, the paths of Christ in the Gospel, we see that there are two ways from Judaea to Galilee. One was busy, more pleasant to travel, less dangerous and shorter. The other was a detour. The longer, more dangerous one, that he actually chose was the one that led him to this encounter with the sinner, the Samaritan woman by the fountain. He chose precisely this way because he was seeking her.

When we say that Christ begs for our love, we mean also that we are free to reject his love. But we must note at the same time the aristocratic reserve of God. He does not ask for our love through great miracles, through astonishing signs of his omnipotence. He did not call down a fire from heaven. He woos us through his pure being; by simply standing there, kindly, simply and understandingly. Defenceless and ready to give himself. Someone could have spat in his face. Why? Because he did not want to dazzle us with his power, because he wanted to have our love in a way that was truly free. In the greatest moment in the history of the world, when he became man, in the annunciation to Mary, a man had to say "yes", in full freedom so that the incarnation was able to be possible at all.

If a beggar is rejected, he generally does not come back. But Christ comes back. He comes again. He will come again at our death in dazzling clarity, but also again in the form of a beggar. God has created us twice: once out of his overflowing love, and a second time and fully in his boundlessly mysterious decision to make his Son beg for our love.

This is also our Christian destiny: to give and beg. To give a present so that others can give us something. God wants us to beg others for things. He asks us to let our humility take on the form of a beggar. In all the situations of life. Even if our love is rejected. We must stick to it, we must not harden our hearts, we must give others new presents, and invent possibilities of continuing to do them good, without them noticing. We remain beggars. What humility the Lord leads us into!

What, then, does Christian humility mean? It means to endure God as he is. This means:

> to bear the darkness of our world and patiently transform it into light;
> to be silent and in this silence to find a good word for others; to realize an essential peace in our restless existence, and to radiate it into the world;
> to confess that we are unworthy and to recognize that in this confession lies our true dignity;
> to see ourselves as beggars in order to be able to give to others.

Basically, humility is the experience that one's own unworthiness, simply admitted, turns into worthiness. By confessing oneself a sinner, one becomes pure. This is the ultimate adventure of our broken existence, the fundamental experience of grace.